I Think ...
I Like You Better ...
Dead

Our spiritual memoir ...

DEDICATION

This book is dedicated to
John's family,
Jodi, Alexandria, and Samantha,
and John's plentiful world of friends.
The spiritual joy I experience in the
non-physical world
is their incredible loss in the physical one.
For this my heart will always be heavy.

*We don't continue relationships
with our loved ones who have died
because we don't expect to.*

Esther Hicks from the Teachings of Abraham
https://www.abraham-hicks.com/

Inspired by these words from Abraham I found myself open to an "afterlife" relationship with my brother John. Then, shortly after his death, the following message was clearly revealed to me through a session with a Medium: *Keep me real. Sometimes, I am standing right beside you. I haven't gone anywhere. Just keep me real.*

Over the next two years, I navigated through my grief, doubt, and fear to do just that. The result is the spiritual memoir.

Is it real … or imagined? I can't say for sure. What is true, however, is that quantum physics has shown the mind does not know the difference.

I chose to believe that the adventures, initiations, and healings we experienced together *were* real.

Will you do the same? Will you let yourself believe that perhaps the book you now hold in your hands, is not so much about our story as it is an invitation … an invitation from a loved one on the other side .. who may be calling you to do the same?

Cathryn 11/6/2020

Endorsement

In this book Cathryn brings into focus that wonderful endeavor of 'partnering' with a deceased beloved in the worlds of spirit. This IDEA of PARTNERING with loved spirit beings to evolve oneself, in order to serve the light of the universe ... is the new spiritually upgrading shortcut at this time on Earth. Cathryn's book demonstrates exactly this important opportunity as a joyful spiritually accelerating strategy.

Alicia Power, Master Intuitive
https://www.soulmentoring.com/

COMMENTS FROM COLLEAGUES

At the beginning of each chapter, you will read a "Comment from a Colleague." I chose to present them to you in the way I received them ... sporadically sprinkled through this experience.

Their encouragement inspired me to *take a pause* ... to *appreciate* what John and I were creating and *digest* the bigger picture of our experience.

My hope is that these shared comments will inspire you to also pause along the way ... to take a moment to reflect on what you have just read ... to find that place in your heart where our experiences can settle ... and perhaps be received as inspiration through your own Soul, from a deceased loved one, who is reaching out to you through our story.

ACKNOWLEDGEMENTS

First, to John's family and friends ...

I cannot begin to acknowledge those who have been instrumental in the creation of this book without first acknowledging those in John's world who had to confront the grief of losing a husband, a father, or close friend ... and my own sister, Suzy, and my brother, Tom, who experienced with me, our shared grief of losing our baby brother ... as well as to their children, and the children of their children, who with varying degrees of closeness, grieve the death of their uncle.

To each of you I must say: I will be forever aware that the joy I have experienced in my continued relationship with John in the spiritual world is your incredible loss in the physical one. Throughout the writing of our memoir, I never lost sight of your pain. And whether this is a real or imagined story, my hope is that at some point it may invite, in some small way, a fond memory, or at least conjure up a smile of times gone by.

For me ... it took a village ... To all in my world, who supported me through John's illness, death, and the evolution of the relationship we share in this story, I am forever grateful. Throughout the pages of our memoir you will read "comments from colleagues". I again chose to present them to you in the way I received them... sporadically sprinkled through this experience ... each being offered at the exact moment I was in need of encouragement, support, or just a need to be believed.

However, beyond my colleagues were those special angels in my life that deserve further acknowledgement.

To Jennifer Forest, Donna Harris, Melanie Kult, Laura Ocampo, and Darlene Turner ... for each being there in your own unique way, to read the latest version ... to hear the most recent adventure. Not only did you validate my experience, you offered the feedback and constructive criticism that kept me motivated to plunge through each version of this truth. But even more than that, each of you were there to support me as I moved through the layers and layers of grief, disbelief, and joy that seasoned this endeavor. Without your daily support I could have. at any moment, abandoned this project out of fear of judgment, ridicule, or shame.

To Jack Pierce, who not only lent his graphic expertise but was there to attentively listen to each twist and turn with an enthusiasm and interest that validated the worthiness of telling the story. And I must thank Robert Allan Arno for his suggestion to change just that one word – the word that softened the entire title!

To Russell and Brian Mariani, and Megan Moore, for your weekly *Coffee House Virtual Gathering*, which not only has given, and continues to give, so many of us a way to move through the isolation of this incredible time on our planet, but also gave me such a supportive forum to speak and share "my truth."

To Hal Zina Bennet who was there when I wrote my first book and has been there through the writing of every book since. I could not be more honored to have your foreword introduce the reader to this work.

To Aaron Leth, the son of my childhood friends, who applied his editorial talents to each word with perfection. Where on earth were you when I wrote my other six books? Your interest, patience, and sincere appreciation for this endeavor fed a part of my Soul that would have otherwise been left unnourished.

I also humbly offer my gratitude to Echo Bodine, Christine Day, and Alicia Power, not only for your contributions to *my* life, but for the incredible gifts you have given, and continue to give, to our world. My gratitude extends, as well, to the members of my Spiritual Group. You joined me during the pandemic crisis for the journey through Alicia Power's work. It is so true that "we teach what we need to learn." Not only was Alicia gracious in condoning my offering her recordings to this group, but those of you who attended gave me the opportunity to take what I was experiencing in my very personal journey and guide each of you through your own expansion and growth.

And then there are those few who not only enriched this project but enrich my life beyond measure. I am blessed to share rich relationships with each of my nieces and nephews, but as is evident in the telling of this story, there was a special bond with my nephew, Sean Tabor. I will forever be grateful for our shared moments of support and encouragement.

And to Lilian Berger, my Godchild, my illuminating angel … you were there in your infancy when I wrote my *Inner Child Workbook*, and now, thirty years later, have been there just as strongly through this experience with my brother.

And of course, I have so much appreciation for, you, Averee, my most constant and loyal canine companion. Morning after morning I would light a candle and go into my daily meditations. You would nap at the end of the bed faithfully holding vigil as John and I went on our elevator excursions and later, as I wrote word after word of our journey.

But to you, my beloved Arthur, I am so grateful for your continued enthusiasm, laughter, support … your ability to tease me out of my collapses down those rabbit holes of despair or disbelief and your willingness to accompany me through hours and hours of tapping from my grief, doubt, and fear to this incredible expansion and joy. But most specifically for being the person that you are … the husband that you are … who, after listening to a poignant part of John's and my story, could turn to me that day, and say, "Just imagine how cool it's going to be when one of us dies …" with such joy and truth that only two who love each other beyond the limitations of their earthly relationship could speak and hear those words with such unadulterated appreciation, anticipation, and joy of what we truly believe is yet to come.

And last, but not least, to all those known and unknown in the world of the unseen … I am so indebted to you, John, for choosing to show up for the contract of our Souls and accompanying me on this journey. To my Guardians, the *infinite intelligence* called "Abraham" for all your teachings, and to all those loved ones in my life who are already on the other side … and those supporting John on his journey … thank you for lending us your support. It truly was and continues to be a building of the bridge between the dimensions that not only changed *our* world but can now be a *call to service* for those on both sides to come and join in the saving of Mother Earth, herself. It does indeed take a village. I feel so blessed to have finally found my tribe.

CONTENTS

FOREWORD:
HAL ZINA BENNETT

Best-selling author of *THE LENS OF PERCEPTION: A USERS GUIDE TO HIGHER CONSCIOUSNESS*

I S IT POSSIBLE to communicate with our loved ones after death? In this intimately written autobiography, the author shares her experiences following the death of her brother John, from whom she'd sadly been estranged for much of their adult life. Surprisingly, her grieving, combined with her desire to heal the relationship they had during their life together before his death, slowly transforms into long discussions with him from *the other side*. He tells her, "I am often standing right next to you. We do connect Soul to Soul."

While deeply moved by her brother's words, Cathryn, a psychotherapist, bestselling author, and longtime student of metaphysics, still has questions about the nature of these communications with John. What is their source? Are these communications real? In life, she and John had once enjoyed a closeness and understanding that she misses. One of the things they had shared in life was that they were both highly imaginative. Could that be the source of their connection now? Was John in his present post-death form only the product of her own imagination. Or, was this mental ability that they both possessed the link that bridged the two worlds?

Motivated in part by lingering doubts, Cathryn turns to a famous psychic to aid her in her search for answers — be it confirmation of the paranormal, or perhaps other understandings of her experiences. What results from this meeting is a series of startling insights that lead both author and reader to a deeper appreciation of our spiritual as well as physical lives.

In a kind of reversal of roles, John becomes the author's ambassador, with lessons from the *other side.* In addition, he explains how the things he and Cathryn share are important not only to the two of them but to consciousnesses living both in our Earthbound life and in the world where John now exists.

He tells her, at one point, "for now, what you and I are doing is figuring out how I can speak through you — how we can bridge that gap between the two worlds."

What Cathryn and John ultimately *figure out* is how to bring their two worlds together through the writing of this book. In these pages, they in fact do bridge the gap John describes. The insights and observations they share, both in life on THIS SIDE and in life on the other, take us into realms of consciousness that are rare, exciting, and applicable in the continuum of life on both sides of the veil.

Does the book answer every question we might have about life and death? If it doesn't, it certainly narrows that gap John speaks of.

And if you are asking if Cathryn and John's writing this book together healed their relationship, or perhaps created new areas of conflict, which so often happens in creative collaborations, read on. But here's a hint: The title of the book, which came through this collaboration, tells in an ironic way, how their once-strained relationship was transformed. In a humorous, ironic tone that John and she had always shared in their physical life, she tells him, "I think ... I like you better dead." And that, they agree, laughingly, should become the title of this book.

There are other books written about the afterlife and the next dimension of the soul's journey, but I have never read an account so deeply personal and relatable. I didn't just feel that I got to know Cathryn and John Taylor, I caught glimpses of my own soul's journey. I felt an eager beckoning to me from my own higher consciousness; to let go of any misconceptions from the past and to accept a new invitation from a new dimension of my expanded life journey that was going to be kind, compassionate, generous, insightful, healing...and most surprising of all...fun.

Russell Mariani, co-founder: The Center for Functional Nutrition;
author: Principle Eating: The No Diet Way to Complete Health.
https://www.thecenterforfunctionalnutrition.net/

PROLOGUE:
THE CELEBRATION OF A
JOB WELL DONE

I BEGAN MY DAY as usual … making my first cup of tea, letting our dog, Averee, out for his morning relief, then sitting at our dining room table preparing for my morning meditation. This recharge had become as routine as charging my cell phone each night. I'd "plug" into this beam of light, and energy would begin to surge through my body harmonizing my vibration to align with my Higher Self. I would then imagine standing in front of an elevator with complete confidence that my brother would be waiting on the other side of those doors.

Talk about a quintessential long-distance relationship … John had been dead for over a year, but we had become quite accustomed to meeting this way. And I never knew what was in store for our training that day, but John would always give me a clue in the way he was dressed.

If it was going to be a fun-filled day of exploration he would greet me in his "Harvey the invisible rabbit" suit. John played "Harvey" in his high school play. He had used this image as evidence it was truly him the *first* time I met with a Medium after his death. The image of Harvey had become his calling card and

1

we'd both chuckle as we anticipated an adventure. However, if it was to be a day the Spiritual Teachers were going to "school" us on the techniques of alignment and cross-dimensional communication; he would be casually dressed in khaki shorts and a polo shirt. But ... if he was dressed more formally ... I knew a meeting had been scheduled with a higher echelon of Spiritual Beings who would be initiating us in a new dimensional level.

I had no indication as to what level of consciousness the training would target. I just knew that as *my* Guidance meticulously adjusted my attire to ensure I would be appropriately dressed for the occasion, I was to get "reverently ready" to be illuminated, expanded, and transformed.

However, this higher level of training had not started until about a year after John died. There was a series of progressive alignments that had to occur as we learned how to "bridge the gap" between the two worlds and vibrationally acclimate to each other's energy field – him on that side and me on this one. Then ever so slowly we began to be assisted, instructed, and vibrationally aligned in finding ways to not only meet at the veil between the physical and non-physical worlds, but to cooperatively co-exist in both of them. He was introduced as my Ambassador. I was relieved of my duty as his metaphysical guide. The roles were adjusted as I became his portal to this world, while he became my periscope to his.

But on this particular morning, John was grinning at me like a Cheshire cat. He was dressed in casual attire and announced with great joy, "You won't believe what they have in store for us today, Cath! Today ... there will be a celebration. We finished! We did it! Our two-year project has been *approved*! And my Guides just told me the celebration will include their *giving us* the official title of our book!"

I was both excited and confused, "Wait, what? Approved ...

it needed approval? And the title of our book ... *they* give us the title?"

"Well, yes and no ... remember, this book is already in print up here. You and I just had to align enough to live it ... and download it ... so it could materialize in your third dimension. So, *they* won't actually 'give' us the title *per se*. *They* will 'reveal' the title to us."

I had to ponder this for a minute: yes, we *had* finished our two-year project. We *had* completed the multidimensional journey our Souls planned long before we met in this lifetime as Cathy and John, as brother and sister. Indeed, we *had* succeeded ... and *had* cause to celebrate. But I hadn't anticipated an "official" initiation.

"Yes", John continued. "the destiny of our book is already in motion. I mean it's phenomenal ... the marketing team has been selected ... the distribution has been determined. Even the final publisher has been chosen. But once it's in print, Cath, it'll be out of our hands. We were just the stewards of the project. The book has its unique destiny. We just have to get out of its divine way!"

"Well, do *you* know the title?" I asked anxiously.

"Nope, don't have a clue. But, come on, jump in, let's see where they take us for the celebration," John replied.

Interesting, I thought. So, he's just as much in the dark as I am.

The elevator came to a soft stop. The doors slowly opened, and there we were standing at the doorway of Garwood's ... our family's favorite restaurant ... located on the shores of North Lake Tahoe. It had changed management over the years, and of course there had been name changes. But by and large, the establishment remained the same and for decades had been the location of many family events.

John looked at me with child-like glee. "How perfect they selected this spot for our celebration." I smiled and nodded as we were greeted by the staff and escorted to one of our favorite tables on the deck. And this deck ... it looked out over the calming waters of the lake and never failed to offer a sense of majestic connection. Like a life review, the multiple experiences I had encountered over the years while standing on the shores of this lake flooded my consciousness.

But now, here John and I sat, once again, meeting at the veil of the two dimensions. We ordered a beer and toasted each other for a job well done. We joked about the many adventures we'd encountered, before and after, his death. We acknowledged the hardships; laughed at the mishaps; and marveled, with awe, at where we'd been taken and the promise of what was ahead.

Pausing for a moment to gaze out at the water, we both reflected on what this moment truly meant. John then broke the silence. "It's been pretty amazing, Cath ... the way you've shown up for all of this. Thanks for hanging in there ... for trusting me ... for keeping me real. I know it wasn't easy being my sister. I know sometimes I made it pretty rough.

"Yeah," I replied thoughtfully. "We've sure come a long way from the days when, as your inebriated friend so eloquently said to me at your Celebration of Life, 'I gotta tell ya, Cathy, most of the time John thought you were a real kook!'"

John shook his head in agreement. "Back then ... I just didn't know what I didn't know." He smiled, took a sip of his beer, then continued. "But just think, Cath, how much we have ahead of us."

For a moment, we sat together savoring the moment of gratitude with precious anticipation. I then turned to John and posed a question that resulted in one of the most powerful exchanges of this whole experience. "So, John, who do you think will read this book ... I mean, from your perspective up there, who do you think our story will benefit?" John took a deep breath, thoughtfully looked out over the lake, then turned back and said, "From this side of the veil we can see so clearly what we could not see when we were alive. So many of you suffer. You're not valued or understood, and it's so much more apparent how difficult it is when you choose to walk in the shoes of your Soul.

So many of us up here have such deep regret. We turned away from ourselves and from love itself. Our book illustrates how that divide can be resolved and transcended ... how a bridge *can* be built between the two worlds. It shows the readers that relationships with their loved ones don't have to be over just because their loved one dies. It's that person, Cath, who will be inspired to pick up this book ... that person who is looking for confirmation, for answers, for ways to finish what never got resolved. But beyond that, they will also be shown, that relationships can continue ... they can still be a source of growth and exchange ... for both parties.

I didn't know that before I died. But your willingness to keep me "real," to "believe" I was still there, illustrates how the unconscious can become conscious when egos are dissolved. This is big, Cath. It's going to give hope to a lot of people. And look at how much stronger your relationships, even to your own Guardians and Teachers, were amplified. It's that person that is going to be drawn to our book ... and they may not even know why, at first. But somehow those of us on this side will draw their attention to it, and the rest will just unfold."

We simultaneously reached for our beers and glanced out at the lake. I thought about how many times over these last few years John had surprised me with this newfound depth and knowledge. He was so right ... he had become so much more conscious since he died. As I reflected on that my heart began to fill up with this great big smile and John's infamous, shit-eating grin now spread wide on *my* face. With tongue in cheek I turned to him and said, "Ya know, John, I gotta tell ya, I think ... I like you better ... *dead*!"

We both laughed so hard we spit beer all over ourselves. Until ... suddenly ... time stopped. The moment froze. Our mouths opened in disbelief. In drop dead seriousness we simultaneously exclaimed: "That's it ... that's the title of our book!" The name had not been *given* to us. The book simply *revealed* itself to us. And we knew, in that instant, the title was perfect. It captured everything reverent and irreverent we had learned, and were now ready to release and share...

PART ONE:
LIFE, DEATH, AND AFTERLIFE

Cathryn's book is a powerful story with transparency, family dynamics, loaded with amazing insights into the reality of how our souls evolve in the spirit world and here on earth. What a great platform for you and John to awaken the world to who we are so that we better understand the mysteries of life, death, and the continuum.

Wes Hamilton, Master Numerologist, https://www.weshamilton.com/

Your Thoughts and Comments:

_____

_____

_____

_____

_____

_____

_____

_____

_____

_____

_____

_____

_____

_____

_____

_____

_____

_____

_____

_____

CHAPTER ONE:
THICK AS THIEVES

I NEVER THOUGHT ...

I NEVER THOUGHT MY baby brother would die before me. It just never occurred to me. Like most kids, I often worried about my parent's dying — events that had already come to pass when my brother died. My Dad died in 1988, and Mom died in 2009. But here I was, just nine years after Mom's memorial, greeting childhood friends at a "Celebration of Life" for my baby brother. It was November 16, 2018. John had died ten days earlier.

He had been dealing with chronic health issues for about two years. It started in October 2016, when he underwent open-heart surgery. He initially recovered from that procedure, but then, an unidentified infection developed resulting in his first aneurysm a year later. These medical events fostered increased contact between John and me — more visits, more phone calls, and definitely more discussions — many of them about life, before and after death. I knew we shared similar beliefs when on one such visit he turned to me and said, "You know, Cath, I've thought a lot about death in this last year, and I'm ok with it. I think it will be kind of a cool experience." We both saw death as the next big adventure. So contrary to the grief that most of John's friends and other family members were feeling that day, once I received the call that he'd fallen, and we knew death was imminent, I experienced a sense of joyful anticipation. The loss of him in the physical world had not yet hit me. It made sense. He was 64 years old, I had just turned 70, and we were not an active part of each other's day-to-day worlds. Sure, since his medical crises, we had been much more in contact than in previous years, but that was still mostly by phone calls. I was not stricken by the same gut-wrenching loss his wife, children, and close friends were experiencing. I didn't have to get used to his not being there when I woke up, or to losing a partner, a father, a friend.

My loss was not physical, mainly because during the last year most of my connection with John was in the non-physical. If it wasn't via phone it was in my morning meditations when I would connect Soul to Soul. I certainly felt empathy for their grief. But when I received that final call on November 6, and heard John had taken his last breath, I experienced absolute joy in his release. It was a joy that had been rekindled in the last few years, a familiar joy — one we shared as kids.

THE BEGINNING

The first time I remember feeling that joy was March 16, 1954. I was almost six years old. My sister, Suzy, was nine, and my brother, Tom, was seven. When we woke up that morning, Dad told us Mom had gone to the hospital to "deliver" a baby brother. He announced that he was taking us to see them — but first, we got to go to Jake's Café for pancakes. We never got to go out to breakfast, so this was a big day. I remember feeling very joyful. In my five-year-old mind, I'm not sure if the excitement was related to meeting my new baby brother or to the fact that we were getting to go to Jake's Café for pancakes. I just knew I was excited.

After breakfast, Dad drove us up to this big, old house. We lived in St. Paul, Nebraska. The town did not have an official hospital. Most of the children in town were born in this big house. We entered the front door and stood at the bottom of the long, ominous stairway, almost like it reached all the way to heaven. A nurse walked out from behind a closed door. Swaddled in her arms was this little baby. Dad turned to us and said, "There you go kids. That's your new baby brother, named John." She didn't come down the stairs. We couldn't touch him or see him up close. But there he was. There was our new baby brother. We didn't get to see Mom. She was still recovering. Dad then took us to school. That day in our "share and tell" I told the class that I had a new baby brother *and* that I had gotten to go to Jake's Café for pancakes. It was a big day indeed.

But the bigger day was the day Mom and John came home. A story told repeatedly over the years is when Mom and John came home, she put him in the bassinet and then left the room for a minute. She returned just in time to see all three of us hovered around the bassinet looking at our new brother as one of us said, "Do you think he's the next Jesus?" To this day we each take ownership of that comment (only God knows the truth). But what I do know is that John looked so angelic that it was an obvious deduction for a child's mind to make. And today what I know, with absolute certainty, is that he wasn't....

I do, however, remember being intrigued by John. To a five-year-old, he just seemed like an animated doll. As John got older it became common for Mom to leave a bottle in his crib so when he woke up in the morning, he would be able to eat without waking her up. It was also quite common for Mom to find that I had awakened before either of them and had climbed into his crib to feed him. He was like my personal doll, and I assigned myself the role of taking care of him.

Several years later, before he was attending kindergarten, John caught the chickenpox. Again, I took it upon myself to be his caretaker. I would get up early in the morning before I had to go to school to put calamine lotion all over his irritated body, then rush home after school to do the same. There was this need I had to take care of him — a need that prevailed for the next several decades.

THE LIFE-CHANGING FAMILY EVENT

In 1966, when I was a senior in high school and John was in the seventh grade, an event occurred in our family that forever shaped each of our lives.

Dad had a nervous breakdown.

A series of situations occurred that left Dad feeling helpless and unable to cope. He sank deeper and deeper into a depression. He was inconsolable.

Eventually, Dad was hospitalized and underwent a series of electroshock treatments. They mitigated his pain, but he was never again the same man Suzy, Tom, and I had known in childhood.

To us, Dad was our trustworthy protector — our hero. Suzy and Tom were, for the most part, able to sustain that image of Dad because they had already left for college. But John and I were at formative, although very different, stages of growing up. Our impressions of him were gravely affected and the respective experiences we shared in the months to come impacted us in very distinct, yet different, ways.

My Journey

My entire senior year was spent in fear as a result of Dad's condition. The foundation of my childhood crumbled. As I prepared to enter the adult world I grappled with the collapse of my hero. I had spent hours joining Dad's world. I was truly Daddy's little girl, and I wanted to be just like him. Even into my high school years, when most teens are spending time with their peers, I would meet Dad after school to accompany him on his nightly drive to the farm. He owned a small herd of cattle. It was his hobby — his way of relaxing. Sharing that part of his world was rewarding. But Dad's breakdown made me question every-thing about myself.

His vulnerability became *my* vulnerability. Would I, too, need to be electrically shocked to deal with my pain? The fear of not being able to cope haunted me. I carried it into my four years of college. It followed me when I moved to San Francisco to begin my adult life, and it colored my choice of the man I ultimately married. But that same fear also inspired me. I had this innate need to *understand* the depths of Dad's depression in hopes of warding off the threat of my own. In 1976, just ten years after I had left home, two situations occurred that I believed would ensure my emotional security.

The first was that I met Mel, the man who was to become my first husband. I didn't realize until much later that it's common to choose partners in our adult life that carry the same traits as the adults with whom we were raised. Dad was ill- equipped to deal with the emotional landscape of his life. The same could be said about Mel. I had married a composite of Dad. My need to fix Dad got transferred to my preoccupation with fixing my husband.

Forty years later, we now know a great deal more about co-dependency — the obsession to fix another because the pursuit makes us feel better about ourselves — but back then we didn't. However, some part of me knew I needed more emotional "insurance". I also enrolled in graduate school to study psychology with the hopes of becoming — you guessed it — a Marriage and Family Therapist. With this new man in my life as a fresh focus and my career path secured, I believed I would be exempt from the vulnerabilities of life.

I wasn't successful in fixing my husband or in outrunning the fear of my inability to cope. Within three years we were talking about divorce, a prospect that eroded my personal and professional confidence. How could I be an effective therapist? How could I help other couples when I couldn't even make my own marriage work? Dad's breakdown had been in response to his inability to cope with situations in his own life that rendered him helpless. Now, here I was: responding to this complex situation in my own life the same way.

I felt vulnerable, scared, and alone. I recall I would often sit in the student lounge too self-conscious to speak to anyone. My only comfort was engaging in this fantasy of John walking through that door to surprise me — to "save" me from my despair. There was a part of me that felt he was the only one that could understand the depths of what I felt.

In 1978, it caught up with me. I was preparing to graduate, and Mel and I had filed for divorce. My anxiety and self-doubt became unbearable and I experienced what I later referred to as my *own* mini-breakdown. I wasn't just divorcing Mel; I was walking away from a lifestyle that I was raised to expect. Finding a man and getting married with the promise of having children was just what women were expected to do at the time. But then, on the other hand, I came of age in the 1970's. Living in San Francisco put me in the heart of a cultural revolution.

Located a little over 150 miles south was The Esalen Institute, a retreat center founded by Michael Murphy and Dick Price, which gave birth to the "Human Potential Movement." The Equal Rights Amendment and the Women's Liberation Movement, in one way or another, were challenging the hearts of every woman of my generation. Revolutions were happening all around me offering options that had not been available in previous generations. This further confused the matter. Despite this cultural upheaval that would support a woman's independence, the fact that my marriage "had failed" was devastating.

Finally, I scheduled an appointment with a psychiatrist. I was asking for medicinal help to ease my pain. After hearing my story, she looked me straight in the eye and refused to prescribe medication. "What you're describing is grief and dependency. If I give you this medication, you'll simply get dependent on something else. I want you to take four days, and if you still feel the need to be medicated, I will give you what you want, but I don't believe it's what you need." This psychiatrist saw something in me I couldn't see, and when she did, it gave me the strength to find a different way of resolving depression and despair.

With gratitude and regret I realized I didn't have to shock away my pain. I was living in the mecca of alternative healing which offered options that Dad didn't have. I had choices. And I made those choices and have continued to make them from that day on. Nonetheless, the decisions I made at that time forever shaped the course of my life. I spent the next two decades — until the end of Dad's life — resolving *his* AND *my* emotional breakdowns. Truth be told, I have dedicated my entire professional career to the pursuit of transforming breakdowns into breakthroughs!

JOHN'S JOURNEY

I may have inherited Dad's breakdown, but I'd been able to escape the situation. John inherited Dad's vulnerability and anxiety and was left trying to figure out how to survive it. He spent most of his high school years living in the aftermath of Dad's shock treatments, and many years after, avoiding Dad's breakdown. John was too young to know the father Suzy, Tom, and I knew. His relationship with Dad was still developing. He was entering puberty, that tender age when a boy looks to his father to be the role model for the man he is about to become. That didn't happen for John, and he was acutely aware of that fact.

He often told the story about the day his sophomore class went to the courthouse to participate in "Government Day," a class trip to enact a mock trial in front of a representative judge. Dad was the county attorney, and therefore had the responsibility of playing the judge. John's memory of this situation was that Dad was anxious and scared. His hands shook, and his voice cracked. The experience was humiliating for both. Dad later told me that he knew John did not respect him, and John later confided that he was embarrassed by Dad's weakness.

When John told me that story my heart broke. But it forever cemented why John would say he grew up with a Dad much different than Tom, Suzy, and me. He knew it, Dad knew it, and Mom knew it. The dissonance John felt with Dad combined with the emotional unavailability Mom experienced with Dad resulted in John and Mom relying heavily on each other. For the next four years John became Mom's loyal companion — her confidant and her buffer. He learned to medicate his feelings with food and prided himself on the fact that he could eat more hamburgers than any other person in town.

Nevertheless, the situation and isolation did take its toll. By his junior year John felt depressed and, like me, sought medicinal help. He went to see the same psychiatrist Dad had seen. He wasn't as fortunate as I had been. Dad's psychiatrist didn't have the perspective needed to see something different in John. Without question, he prescribed an anti-anxiety pill that I believe John continued to take for the rest of his life. Therapy was not even considered. It was a small town with few resources. But John needed to talk and, by that time, I had become a good listener.

It didn't matter that I lived in San Francisco and the long-distance charges were significant. John had permission to call whenever he felt the need – and the need was frequent. There was a strong bond, we were the survivors, and we had gone through the ordeal together. Our experiences may have been different, and the roads traveled may have been different, but those differences were the topics of our conversations for many years.

I left the family situation in 1966, and in 1973 John was finally able to do the same. He moved to Lincoln to attend the University of Nebraska. Many of his high school friends enrolled there as well. He had the continuity of his high school cronies and some emotional distance from the situation at home. During his junior year, he met Keri.

Cathryn's story is one that many of us can relate to; Cathryn needed, and had, the courage to stand her ground while staying open. We all go through those times when our family thinks we are crazy, reading this book made me appreciate how to deal with those situations from a different point of view. I would recommend this book as being both thought provoking and emotionally touching.

Don Snyder, Akashic Records Reading and Healing
https://www.donaldjsnyder.com/

Your Thoughts and Comments:

_____

_____

_____

_____

_____

_____

_____

_____

_____

_____

_____

_____

_____

_____

_____

_____

_____

_____

_____

_____

_____

CHAPTER TWO:
STRAINED, ESTRANGED —
THEN SEPARATE

A DIVORCE AND AN ENGAGEMENT

JOHN HAD TOLD me about Keri, a fellow student. Keri was John's first "real" girlfriend, and he was enchanted. I was excited when he told me she would be coming to San Francisco with him to celebrate Christmas with our family. It was 1977. Mel and I — who, by that time, were *unhappily* married — had volunteered to pick them up at the airport. It was pre-9/11, so we could still meet loved ones at the gate when the plane arrived. I was ecstatic to see John. The minute I saw him I ran up to him, screaming and yelling as I gave him a huge bear hug. The excitement was genuine and natural for John and me — but for Keri it was overwhelming.

When John and I had a moment alone he told me that she did not know what to do with my *overzealousness,* nor our closeness. I wasn't sure what that meant. But Keri was important to John. Of course, I wanted her to like me. I felt confident that we would find a way to bridge any differences that existed between us.

Over the next several years, it became obvious this was not the case. Slowly, I sensed John pulling away from me. It became excruciatingly evident why on June 9, 1978, my 30th birthday. John and Keri had recently gotten engaged. And I had recently started the process of filing for divorce. When I went to the mailbox I found an envelope from John. It wasn't a birthday card as expected. It was a letter. I felt curious and excited. Maybe, I thought, *maybe* we're finally going to get back on track.

Instead, it said, "I'm sorry you are going through such a rough time with your divorce ... but Keri doesn't like my melancholy side that comes out when I relate to you, so I can't be there for you in the same old way. You're strong and have a lot of support. I know you will get through this." He continued to say that one of the things he liked about Keri was that she didn't let things "get to her" and she was encouraging him to be the same way.

I wasn't sure what the ramifications of his choice would be. The budding therapist within me understood and accepted how he felt without question. Our respective journeys *were* different. While I was diving into the emotional aftermath of our shared experience, John was trying to move on from it. And I did have support from the students/friends I had met in graduate school. But there was also the part of me who sat in that student lounge hiding out in the fantasy of his rescuing me from my marital despair. That part of me was crushed and felt even more abandoned and alone.

Our closeness progressively dissolved. It became more and more obvious that not only did John *not* want to be around my melancholy side — he didn't particularly care to be around me at all. He began to take on this air of superiority. When I *was* around him — and especially around the two of them together — John was constantly offering *suggestions* on how I *should* be living my life differently. He was, and often they both were, critical of my bohemian style of dress, the way I ran my business, as well as my finances and love life. At one particular family gathering, John turned to me and offered to give me $200 if I would just go to the Gap and get some *decent* clothes. It was insulting. I loved the way I dressed, but began to dread being around him.

It came to a head one night in the early 1980's when our family met in Omaha to celebrate Christmas. John and Keri had been married for several years, and I had been divorced for about the same time. We were all sitting in the bar having a drink before our dinner reservation. I was sitting next to Dad, who was wearing his favorite hat. I grabbed it and plopped it on my head, teasing that it completed my outfit. Keri disapprovingly quipped, "You'll never find a man again dressing like that."

Still reeling from the tail-end of my divorce, I was not in the mood for such a snarky comment. It just hit me the wrong way. I snapped back, "Fuck you." I lost my appetite, stood up, gave Dad's hat back to him, and left the bar to join my sister's two children Michelle, ten, and Sean, eight, for dinner.

The next morning I hoped I would avoid seeing anyone because I had booked an early flight back to California. However, when leaving to catch the airport shuttle at my hotel, John was already in the lobby drinking a cup of coffee. We didn't speak. I had several bags. When he saw me struggling, he carried the heavier bag to the van, turned around and walked away without even saying goodbye. As I lifted my second bag to the last step, I muttered to myself, "I am *never* spending holidays with John and Keri again." I was furious and hurt. I'm not sure what John felt, but I know he felt something because, other than one significant phone call, we didn't speak again with any depth for almost eight years. However, due to a turn of events I could have never predicted, the truth is that between that family gathering and the death of our father, there were few opportunities for connection.

THE BANISHMENT: GUESS WHO'S COMING TO DINNER?

Contrary to Keri's prediction, I *did* find a man. It happened one October day in 1983. I was attending a professional conference in Washington, D.C., and had gone out for a morning jog. As I was running along the tree-lined path of the National Mall, my eye caught a glimpse of this man sitting on a bench reading a book. He didn't seem to notice me, but something kept drawing me back to him. It was like this force of nature that seemed bigger than my own will. I looped back, stopped in front of him, and asked if I could sit down. I'd never done anything like that before — my behavior was completely foreign to me.

We talked for several hours. I realized when I walked away, we hadn't exchanged names. I *had*, however, given him the phone number where I could be reached. Sure enough, he called later that day. His name was Walter. We spent the next several days getting to know each other. When I returned home, we kept in touch by letters. As it turned out he was at a crossroads in his life. One thing led to another and by that following January, he decided to relocate to California. It gave us the opportunity to get to know each other even better.

That following March, I flew back to Nebraska to see my family. Mom picked me up at the airport. On our half-hour drive home I excitedly told her I had started dating a man that I really liked. She was pleased. Then I said rather casually that he was Black. There was no way I was prepared for her response. She was silent for a moment and then said, "I was always afraid of this. It's as if you just stabbed me in the heart."

I was shocked. I had no point of reference for her remark. True: growing up in the middle of Nebraska did not lend itself to a cross-cultural experience, but I had never witnessed Mom being uncomfortable around anyone of color. However, she *was* definitely uncomfortable with my news, and there was certainly no room for discussion. Instead, there was a cold, still silence for the rest of the drive. When I told Dad, he winced and then said, "Well, I guess it's okay as long as you don't marry." Those were the last words Dad spoke directly to me about the situation.

The next few years were strained in ways I could have never imagined. John and Keri's criticisms paled in comparison to Mom and Dad's rejection. This was acutely obvious on April 25, 1984. I woke up and flipped on the television to catch the morning news. Much to my astonishment, I heard the news commentator announce my hometown had been hit by a severe tornado. St. Paul, Nebraska, is a town of around 2000 people. It's not every day it makes the national news. My heart skipped a beat. I immediately called home to make sure everyone was okay.

Mom answered. When she realized it was me, the tone of her voice changed — she became curt and to the point. She assured me they were okay, and then I heard her say to Dad, "Chuck, it's Cathy, do you want to speak to her?" I didn't hear his response, but Mom returned to the phone and said, "Okay, thanks for calling, there are other calls I have to make," and abruptly hung up. It was the first time in my life my father refused to speak with me. It was like getting shot in the heart with a stun gun.

Several weeks later I received a phone call from a family friend. "So, Cathy, what are you going to do about this? Do you realize how much you are hurting your parents?" I'd grown up knowing this man. He was well-respected in our community — and *I* respected him. But I could only reply by saying, "Otto, I'm really sorry they are so hurt, but I just can't live my life according to their prejudices. That's just not who I am."

A few days later there was another unexpected phone call. This time it was John. It took me by surprise, but he launched right into the conversation by saying, "I just want you to know that Mom and Dad are talking about taking you out of the will. I told them I thought that was stupid, and I would never support it." There was no room for a response other than to tell him I appreciated that. One thing I can say about John is that he had a strong moral compass. And I must admit it felt wonderful to have "the brother that I knew" show up in my defense.

In the winter of that year, the family had reservations to meet in Colorado for Christmas. I had purchased my tickets months in advance. In November I received a letter from Mom "uninviting" me. "It's just too stressful to be around you," it read. Over the next several years holidays came and went. Mom's seventieth birthday came and went, and I continued to be excluded. My concern about the underlying tension experienced when I was around John and Keri took a dramatic backseat to what I now felt in response to being "officially" banned from family gatherings. Over the next several years I had no contact with them ... so my relationship became irrelevant.

However, I did remain close to my sister Suzy and her family. We both lived in California, and I was very close to her children. In fact, Walter and I spent a great deal of time with Sean and Michelle. And my brother Tom did meet Walter when he came to visit, but, other than that, contact with the family radically diminished. And as it did, Keri's involvement became more pronounced. It felt as though I was slowly being replaced.

TAKE YOUR STAND & STAY OPEN

In hindsight, perhaps the biggest relationship affected was my relationship with myself. I struggled to keep my heart open. It didn't feel right to counter their rejection with judgment. But walking both sides of this conflict — pursuing the relationship with Walter while at the same time remaining hopeful that Mom and Dad would change their position — was emotionally challenging. Oddly enough, the conference in Washington, D.C., I had attended the previous year gave me the inspiration to do just that.

It was the annual *Marriage and Family Therapy Conference*. The topic presented in one of the breakout sessions discussed the development of one's "individual character." The presenter shared a poignant story about being offered a once-in-a-lifetime career option that required her to commute from Washington, D.

C., to Boston. She was the mother of three young children. Accepting the position would create difficulty. She shared how empowering it had been when she simply stated her situation to her family with no preconceived idea of how they might respond. "I didn't try to get them to agree with my choice. I simply *took my stand and stayed open."* Much to her surprise, her family was able to reach a solution upon which they all agreed. She encouraged each of us to do the same when confronted with a conflictual, and potentially difficult, situation.

I can't tell you how many times I used the phrase "take my stand and stay open" as my mantra. Her words inspired me to take my stand with my parents without judgment of their response. I *hoped* they would accept my choice, but I *strived* to keep my heart open to them even if they didn't. Somehow this enabled me to navigate through myriad feelings that accompanied my conviction and their rejection. I could have become angry and spouted ultimatums to match their threats, but I just never let myself go to that place. It helped that I had a lot of support from Walter. He greatly valued family and encouraged me to not turn my back on my parents. He always said, "It's just not right."

We were able to hold this posture with each other as well, and to our credit, we courageously navigated through their racism with humility and grace. In fact, in some ways, their rejection strengthened our bond. It forced conversations that invited us to confront and resolve feelings that may not have otherwise emerged.

Cohabiting in Marin County, California, a progressive community located north of San Francisco, also made it easier. It was 1984. Bi-racial couples were part of the norm. Although other issues did emerge between us, we both agree (even now in 2020 amidst the racial unrest that's so prevalent) that race was never one of them. It was as if we existed within this protective bubble that provided the exact environment we each needed to evolve individually and grow as a couple.

But, when I reflect back on that time now, what's even more amazing is how staying true to my convictions without reacting or rebelling contributed to the development of my character, built my integrity, and laid the groundwork for my capacity to forgive. Without these experiences and the lessons I learned in response to my relationship with Walter, to Mom and Dad's rejections, and even to John and Keri's criticisms, I would have never been inspired — or forced — to develop the skills needed to stay present with an open heart.

This evolution occurred through what I can now identify as four major milestones. Each milestone ultimately and collectively became the foundation for my ability to repair the relationships with Mom, Dad, and even John, as well as becoming the major building blocks for the method of healing I developed and have offered to my client base for the last 40 years.

CHARACTER-BUILDING MILESTONES
1ST MILESTONE: REJECTION BUILDS CHARACTER

This first milestone was a direct result of the rejection I experienced with Mom and Dad. Their reaction to my choice in a partner forced a new action within me based on conviction, integrity, and faith. The result was the emergence of an adult self that progressively evolved as I maintained my resolve with Mom and Dad. The key component again, however, was the fact that I did so while sustaining an open heart. I continued to hold hope that their position might change. Dealing with this challenge empowered the adult part within me that learned how to endure, navigate, and process strong emotion without shutting down. This required me to not only *define* my values, but also to find the courage needed to *stand by* these values. Flexing that muscle strengthened my character more than any prior life experience — even that of Dad's nervous breakdown when I was seventeen.

2ND MILESTONE: PERCEIVED ABANDONMENT INSPIRES ACCOUNTABILITY

But, surprisingly, the second most profound *character-building* milestone occurred in response to an issue Walter and I confronted. It was one that could not be addressed while in relationship with each other. From the moment Walter crossed the country from Washington, D.C., to San Francisco, he struggled with being so far away from his young three children. The day came when he realized he needed to return to address this separation – which meant leaving our relationship, and me, with no guarantee that he would return. I, of course, supported his decision but felt tremendous sadness and grief at the prospect of losing him. I was still dealing with the rejection of Mom and Dad. Facing the possibility of losing Walter was more than I could bear.

And it wasn't as if I could run back to them now that the relationship might not work. Dealing with their rejection was not relevant to whether our relationship worked. Other than my sister and her family, I wasn't in contact with them at that time. It was clear to me that the situation between Walter and me *did not* impact the situation between me and them. But I was in pain, and I definitely needed support in figuring out how to manage that pain.

A good friend of mine suggested I schedule an appointment with Darlene, an intuitive healer. She felt Darlene might be able to offer a fresh perspective – and that she did. After listening to me "tell my tale," Darlene simply said, "There is a little girl inside you who feels rejected and alone. Go home and sit in front of the mirror. Rock back and forth as you comfort her and tell her she is safe and loved."

I was a family therapist. I knew how to help family members speak to each other — and moreover, hear and comfort each other. But I was also acutely aware of the fact that the only reason I could now do this for my inner child was because I had sustained my integrity with Mom and Dad. I was believable. I was trustworthy. I knew how to make that child within me feel safe. And I did just that. I built a relationship with her by always showing up for her. Whenever I felt overcome with sadness or grief, I would sit in my rocking chair and rock back and forth. I held her and comforted her and walked her through her pain.

And it worked. It worked every time. Initially, I spent *hours* in front of the mirror rocking, comforting, self-soothing, as I moved from a blaming and shaming paradigm to one of complete self-responsibility. The intense emotion would subside, and as it did, the thought of Walter leaving became less and less devastating. I trusted I would be okay, and my inner child learned to *trust* I would *make sure* she was okay. I didn't have to blame Walter for my pain or resent him for his choice when in June 1985, he did leave California to return to Washington, D.C.

We agreed to sever all contact so he could determine his best course without our relationship deterring him. Once he was gone, I witnessed the power of this technique even more. I felt no blame — shame — or guilt. Addressing my grief by *responding* to it instead of *projecting* it onto Walter and resenting him was life empowering. Eventually this method of managing feelings expanded beyond the absence of Walter. It extended to similar feelings from my past.

Sometimes it felt as though every experience of abandonment, betrayal, and rejection was being dislodged. Feelings from Dad's breakdown came back — pain from John's letter and subsequent dismissal re-emerged — and most definitely additional layers of Mom and Dad's rejection surfaced and needed to be addressed. But I was able to remain steady and "rock" my way through each emergence of feelings. This success bolstered my self-esteem and motivated me to further commit to mastering this technique. And even though that "mastery" (which is ongoing) did not come easily, it soon became the foundation for my entire career.

3RD MILESTONE: MY SOUL SPEAKS AND DISPELS ISOLATION AND LONELINESS

I had learned how to rescue my inner child but, just as amazing was the fact that I also began to hear the voice of my Higher Self: the voice of my Soul. It was serendipitous, but gradually I began to sense this loving presence around me. As I comforted my inner child, my Soul was comforting me. The focus of energy shifted from my relationship with Walter, or even relationship situations from my past. It became more about solidifying the "vertical" relationship among these three aspects of me: my inner child, my inner adult, and my Higher Self, or Soul. The construction of this internal relationship provided a security I had never known. My inner child could rely on me, and I could rely on my Higher Self or Soul. I increasingly became more and more capable of *responding* to the events in my life as opposed to *reacting* to them.

4TH MILESTONE: THERE'S MORE THAN MEETS THE HUMAN EYE

This alignment inspired me to explore the spiritual purpose of specific life experiences — with Mom and Dad, as well as the recent situation with Walter. This development added an entirely new dimension to my relationships and to the experiences I had in response to those relationships.

By the time Walter returned to California — which he did six months later — we had both changed. He had made as much peace with his relocation as he could, and my capacity for *embracing* difficult feelings had expanded beyond present day situations. We resumed our relationship on this new fertile ground. I was going in a more metaphysical direction, which we had not really explored before he left. But I was beginning to incorporate this line of thinking more and more into my daily challenges. He wasn't as enthused as I was with this line of thinking, but gratefully, he was willing to look at specific facets of our relationship from this perspective.

I had already deduced that the attraction Walter and I felt toward each other the day we sat on the bench at the National Mall was evidence of a spiritual connection. We both experienced what's known as *soul recognition* — the feeling of familiarity, or of knowing someone intimately even though you just met them for the first time.

But even *before* I met Walter, I had been exchanging sessions with a college friend who was researching past life regression. My continued work with her sparked my exploration of past life influences on present-day situations even further. This led to a series of otherworldly explorations that deepened the relevance and understanding of the dynamics within our relationship. But it also served to help us better understand that initial response Mom had to our relationship that had always puzzled me.

Now keep in mind that Walter left and returned with only my sister knowing about the situation. So even though there was a break in our relationship, there had not been a break in Mom and Dad's reaction to us as a couple. As our relationship resumed, so did our need to confront their continual rejection. Mom's initial comment when I told her about my relationship with Walter, and the fact that he was Black, had always left me dumbfounded. When I considered her comment as a possible past life response I was even further intrigued. What did the statement, "I was always afraid of this ... it's as if you just stabbed me in the heart," even mean? Those words just didn't make sense in this time and place. It left me curious to explore this possible perspective. And I had studied metaphysics enough to understand that every feeling we have, every statement we make, has a context somewhere in time, even when it is not immediately evident.

I appreciated the fact that Walter was willing to explore with me where in our Soul's history Mom's comment might make sense. We hoped that perhaps looking at her words through this metaphysical lens might help us better understand her extreme position. Something always felt off, and I sensed there was more to this than could be seen through the "human" eye.

We simultaneously entered an expanded state of consciousness and asked our Higher Selves to show us any past-life record that may relate to this situation. We both were silent for a moment. Then Walter began seeing in his mind's eye a past life in which Mom and I were again mother and daughter. The terrain was desert-like prairie. There was great tension between the settlers and the indigenous tribes that lived on that land. Some tribes sought justice, while others sought peace. One night there was a raid on our property by a group of rogue rebels. Walter's tribe had come to combat the rebels, but in the crossfire, Mom had been killed by an arrow that pierced her heart. The arrow had come from Walter's hand. It was a mistake, but Mom's Soul left her body carrying that story of the trauma of her death. It was recorded in the DNA of her Soul, and it appeared as though it had followed her into this lifetime.

IT WOULD'VE BEEN WONDERFUL ...

Once this *version of the truth* was revealed, Walter and I opened our eyes and stared at each other in disbelief. Again, I recalled those first words Mom said when I had told her about Walter. "I was always afraid of this. It's as if you just stabbed me in the heart." Seen now, in the context of this past life, those words had an entirely different meaning. Was it possible that Mom was subconsciously responding to this Soul wound with no present-day framework to justify her feelings of terror, other than Walter's race? That question had no answer, but this multi-dimensional perspective did shed important light on this heart-wrenching situation.

And *it would've been wonderful* if this perspective could have been shared with Mom *at the time*. But it wasn't. And *it would've been wonderful* if this version could've invited an entirely different kind of conversation *at that time*. But it didn't.

What *was* wonderful about experiencing this perspective, however, was that it set the stage for my being able to integrate, as well as value, the metaphysical context with regards to my human challenges. In fact, there were a variety of past life situations that provided insight into certain patterns and blocks Walter and I confronted, both together and separately. The fact that we were both willing to look beyond the obvious, and explore our wounded selves as well as the history of our Souls, gave us the foundation we each respectively needed to evolve into the people we are today.

THE END RESULT

The capacity to cope with extreme feelings — inspired by Mom and Dad's rejection — combined with the development of my inner child work and inspired by the break in my relationship with Walter, offered me a way to resolve, with compassion and love, the deep-seated feelings from my past. When I co-mingled the experiences of my current life with those of my past life, I was able to apply the philosophy of "taking my stand and staying open" to even more profound circumstances. This "evolved consciousness" *inspired,* as well as *allowed,* me to learn the power of forgiveness. It is this very combination that enabled me to heal the rejection from John and come back into relationship with him both before, and now after, his death; and to process the incredible banishment experienced with Mom and Dad. It prepared me to stay present in a loving way in my relationship with Walter, and paved the way for my heart to graciously respond to my father's end-of-life transition that temporarily "banished the banishment" and called me back into the "family" circle.

THE BANISHMENT GETS BANISHED

In the spring of 1987, the phone rang. It was Mom. We had not spoken for over a year. She called to tell me that Dad was again suffering from depression. He had been admitted to a psychiatric ward and she thought, because of my profession, I would want to know. The conversation was tense, but she then asked if I would be willing to look at Dad's medical records. I agreed, but with trepidation. I was conflicted about the relationship with Mom. Walter and I had uncovered our past life, but it had not been shared and nothing had changed. I was confused as to how this would impact my relationship with Walter. He and I talked a great deal about the presenting circumstances. I worked with my inner child and consulted with my Soul. The consensus was that it was time for me to step back in.

Once I read Dad's medical records, I contacted several geriatric specialists to research options. They confirmed there were none. I was told that the preferred treatment for someone Dad's age with his presenting problems was again, electroshock therapy. This discovery took me down a very treacherous road. Part of my motivation for becoming a therapist was to ensure that if Dad ever became depressed again, I would be equipped to help him. However, it was becoming more and more obvious that this career choice was also to protect *me* from ever having to re-experience that unbearable feeling of powerlessness I had felt at seventeen.

I was now twenty years older and had been studying psychology for the past ten years. It was heartbreaking to realize those ten years of study didn't prepare me to offer anything new. It was even more infuriating to recognize that in the last twenty years the field of psychology had not advanced at all in this area. However, as the specialists predicted, all interventions we tried failed. Medications didn't work; meetings with psychiatrists didn't work; and admittance to a psychiatric unit with group therapy didn't work.

In November 1987, Dad was again prescribed a series of electroshock therapy. However, this time, as sad as it was, even the shock treatments didn't work. He continued to be riddled with depression and was eventually admitted to the long-term care treatment unit at the local hospital. Over the next few months, he lost all will to live and began to refuse food and water. The medical staff attempted to feed him intravenously, but he violently fought them.

On March 26, 1988, I flew home to Nebraska to assist. It was odd being home after having been so "unwelcomed." Yet, that part of me that *intuitively* knew it was time to step back into the family system prevailed. There was some reason I needed to be there and everything else was simply put on hold.

When I arrived, it was evident Mom and I had declared an unspoken truce. I had not seen Dad for several years. He was half the man he was the last time I saw him. I spent hours sitting by his bedside reflecting on our life together. It was as if every child within said their goodbyes as the adult within me prepared my father for his death.

On March 31, I woke up and went to the hospital. Mom decided to stay home that day saying she needed a break. It had been a long haul for her. Dad's condition had gravely worsened. He was going in and out of consciousness. Tom stopped in and then went to spend the day with Mom. Suzy called and I was able to hold the phone to Dad's ear so she could say goodbye. John arrived around 4 p.m. I jiggled Dad's arm to wake him up. "Dad, Dad, John's here." Dad opened his eyes, looked up, said John's name, and then lapsed back into unconsciousness. He died three hours later. John's name was the last word Dad ever spoke.

Dad's last several months had been hard on all of us, but John was the most unsettled by them. Their relationship was the least resolved, and he was the most troubled by the burden that Dad had become on Mom.

THE TABLES TURN

I returned to California and spent the next four years involved with Walter but, other than my sister and her family, I remained uninvolved with our family. I continued to tend to the needs of my inner child and kept close contact with my Higher Self. Six months after I returned from Dad's death, Walter's dad died. He was as gravely affected by his father's death as I was mine. We were grieving our pasts in our own unique ways.

Even though I had little contact with Mom *after* Dad died, my life's journey had been dramatically impacted *during* those last six days before his death. Being with him at that precious moment of his passing changed me. It had been one thing to *take my stand and stay open* when Mom and Dad were rejecting me. But somehow, staying emotionally present with Dad as he was leaving Earth and actually being able to navigate between all the varied emotions successfully, forced a resolution of all he and I had ever been together. It solidified that bridge between my human experience and my spiritual pursuit. I began to place every experience on this newly developed human/spiritual continuum, weighing the possible lesson of my Soul against the price my human self was having to pay.

One of the primary backdrops of this exploration continued to be the relationship between Walter and me. I scrutinized every turn in our relationship from this perspective. He was a willing participant. Over those next four years the spiritual and psychological weave enabled us as a couple, and as individuals, to navigate effectively through the ensuing issues that emerged. We were graciously (and sometimes, not so graciously) able to explore how we fit together and how we did not. Ultimately, in the summer of 1990, we mutually acknowledged our relationship had served its purpose. There was no blame or shame. It had been a bedrock of healing — an invaluable platform that gave birth to whom we have each become, and to this day, we remain, friends, colleagues, and sources of spiritual support.

My career also matured as I wove the psycho-spiritual tenets into my professional sessions with others. In 1991, I wrote my *Inner Child Workbook*, which was bought, published, and released. Much of the content of the book was inspired by the healing of *my* childhood — and much of that healing came in response to the 20+ years of inner work I had done related to Dad's breakdown and his death; to my rejection and judgment from John, to my banishment from family gatherings; and the life-changing beginnings and endings of my relationship with Walter.

On the Road with My Dog Named Max

By 1993, my book had become a bestseller. I began receiving requests from around the country to offer inner-child workshops, and with all the changes and losses behind me, I was ready for something new. Shortly thereafter, a woman contacted me saying that she loved my book and wanted to know if I would be interested in hiring her to organize a national workshop tour. The details lined up and within eight months I had sold everything, bought an RV, and in January 1994, my dog, Max, and I crossed the Golden Gate Bridge heading east for a yearlong tour to places known and unknown.

Now, I have to tell you that a person doesn't spend a year on a road trip in an RV, with her dog as her only constant companion, without being altered. Granted, I did have contact with the participants in each of the workshops that occurred around the country, but outside of those sessions, I had the choice to either experience great loneliness or to further solidify the relationship with my Higher Self. I used the time to fortify the latter. The publication of my work defined my career path, and my solo adventure gave me ample time to continue down my road of self-discovery — a road that in the end led me to my Souls' other half.

This is a must-read for anyone who has had the experience of losing a loved one, only to find them again in a new dimension; and a must-read for anyone who has a curiosity for such an event. Cathryn tells of her experience with a heartfelt honesty that will surely convince the reader of not just life after death, but of other-worldly guidance available to those of us left behind. A joyful, enlightening read!

Rev. Carl,
Author of the novel & screenplay, "Jesus of Nebraska"
612-600-1402

YOUR THOUGHTS AND COMMENTS:

_____

_____

_____

_____

_____

_____

_____

_____

_____

_____

_____

_____

_____

_____

_____

_____

_____

_____

_____

_____

CHAPTER THREE:
RELATIONSHIPS: NEW AND RENEWED

THE NEW RELATIONSHIP

O UR MEETING WAS, and continues to be, a monumental event in my life and ultimately resulted in an unpredicted move. It is well understood in the psychological community that all relationships, especially ones of a romantic nature, are based on projection. We see in another that which we do not want to see in ourselves. When this dynamic is seasoned with a spiritual component, the projection takes on a more profound significance. Often referred to as "twin flames," a relationship of this caliber offers the strongest mirror available for self-reflection. It is as challenging as it is rewarding. Such was the case the moment I met Arthur.

Arthur was a first-generation immigrant from Poland. He'd moved to the states to pursue his spiritual path. We met in the fall of 1994 in Minneapolis. It was the last leg of my workshop tour. Arthur had signed up for a weekend class I was offering. Over the next several years our relationship evolved. There were hurdles to overcome, and of course challenges to meet, but by 1996, the relationship evolved and resulted in me moving to Minnesota to join him in marriage.

Our union provided a new landscape for reflection. Most of my childhood patterns had been healed, or I at least had acquired the tools to deal with whatever did emerge emotionally. This gave way to explore more deeply the lessons of my Soul. Reactions changed. I became a student, instead of a victim, of my rejections and banishments, my disappointments, failures, and successes. I remained steadfast and responsive to the needs of my children within and viewed the experiences of my life, both past and present, from that multidimensional lens. This was not only most obvious, as well as useful, in my relationship with Arthur, but also greatly impacted how I viewed and experienced the relationship with my family.

A RETURN TO MY ROOTS

And so … after living in California for 27 years I made the unpredicted move back to my roots. Minnesota is considerably closer to Nebraska than California. My return to the Midwest meant I was closer to my family than I had been in years. Because of the scrutiny I had experienced concerning my previous relationship with Walter, I was reluctant to involve my family in this newfound journey. Yet, because of the inner work I had done, I was not opposed to it. Several years into our marriage, an occasion presented itself that offered an opportunity.

Arthur's mother, who lives in Poland, came to visit. She wanted to meet my mother. It was June 1998. By this time, peace had been made on many levels, and I was once again participating — although somewhat reluctantly — in family gatherings. I was getting ready to celebrate my 50th birthday, so I suggested we all meet in Omaha, Nebraska. Arthur, his Mom, and I drove from

Minneapolis. Mom, Tom, and his wife, Pam, lived near enough to meet us, and Suzy flew in from California.

John and Keri lived in Norfolk, Nebraska, a city about an hour from Omaha. I had not had much contact with them in the ten years since Dad's death, but I did extend an obligatory invitation. When Mom relayed that they were unable to come, I was relieved. However, much to my chagrin, they showed up. Keri proceeded to get quite drunk. There was little conversation between John and Keri. This was the first time I had any hint there was tension between them, but it was not the first time I suspected Keri had a problem with alcohol.

Over the next several years it became apparent that the life path John was on was quite different than mine. Whereas I had remarried, I later found out through the family grapevine that they had filed for divorce. I was not privy to the demise of their relationship — nor would it be my story to tell — but a byproduct was that John had the foresight to seek counseling.

RELATIONSHIPS RENEWED

With the support to address his feelings, his heart began to reopen. It was gradual, but as it did, he began to welcome me back into his world.

Another opening took place in the relationship with Mom. During Dad's death and funeral, Mom and I had opened the door to making peace. We hadn't talked directly about their rejection of Walter and me, but by then, eight years later, the circumstances regarding that situation had changed. Walter and I were no longer together, and ... Dad was dead. I had often wondered if Dad was the true racist, and, especially since that past life revelation, if Mom was just following suit. But another situation that supported this possibility was that my niece, Cathy, had married a man of color and had given birth to two children.

Cathy, Pierre, and her two children were well- received with little discussion or judgement? This change of heart set the stage for a reckoning between Mom and me.

It happened partly because my move to Minnesota resulted in more visits to Nebraska. I had high school friends that still lived there, my brother Tom and his family lived near Mom, and John had moved to Omaha after his divorce. Tensions overall had eased. Whenever I was in town, I stayed with Mom. One afternoon Mom and I were watching *Oprah*. The show was featuring children of mixed races. At one point, Mom looked at me and innocently said, "I just don't know what the big deal is." I was astounded. I looked at her and I literally said, "Are you fricking kidding me? Do you have any idea who you are talking to right now? Don't you remember all those years I was not welcomed in your home because of my relationship with Walter?" I wasn't angry or accusatory. I was just truly overcome with disbelief.

Mom paused and looked at me as if I were talking about somebody else. She shook her head in dismay and, honest-to-God said, "I just don't know what that was all about." I took a deep breath and said, "Well I do." And I proceeded to tell her about the past life that Walter and I had uncovered. It was as if I was not even talking to the same woman who had previously been so unwavering in her rejection.

It made me wonder ... was it really Dad's issue that Mom was camouflaging? Was Mom's acceptance of Cathy and her family just an offshoot of Walter and me breaking Mom's racist barrier? Or was it really as simple as a past- life trigger? Her response to Walter and me I deemed racist, but was the context of her feelings from another time and place? Mom's response made me believe even more strongly there was at least, in part, a multidimensional context for her rejection and racism. But again, even though this situation was definitely black and white, there were many shades of gray concerning the respective responses. And no one could deny the shade that touched the lives of Walter and me *at that time* carried scars in this life that were very hard to repair.

SOUL-TO-SOUL ENCOUNTERS

By 2001, my passion for working with the spiritual nature of things had evolved. I was asked to be a featured speaker at an all-day workshop. Dahna Fox was also a featured speaker. She taught people how to access the records of one's Soul. Referred to as the *Book of Life* or the *Akashic Records*, they consist of an energy field upon which the experiences of each Soul are recorded. We immediately took to one another and agreed to exchange services. I facilitated the work with her inner child, and she taught me how to access the Akashic Records — both my own and others.

When I shared this newfound talent with John, he was intrigued. Over the next several years he would often ask me to access his records in response to challenges he was having with being single. His heart was wide open, and the more his heart opened, the more he found his way back to our relationship. At one point, John introduced me to a woman he was dating. After we had talked for a few minutes she looked at John and said, "Boy, John, talking to your sister is like talking to a female version of you." That comment rekindled a familiarity — a likeness — that John and I had not shared for almost 25 years.

In June 2004, the phone rang. It was Gene, Mom's handyman. Mom had fallen and broken her hip. Both John and I were in between jobs at the time, so I drove down from Minneapolis, picked him up in Omaha, and we drove together to central Nebraska to be at the hospital while Mom had surgery. She was hospitalized for the next several weeks. We wanted to be close to her, so John and I spent that time together in our family home.

It was the longest time we had been around each other since childhood.

John and the woman he had been dating had recently ended their relationship. He was emotionally raw. His heart was tender and his confidence tentative, so being with me was comforting. As a *trained* listener, I understood his pain. I had spent my whole life navigating through tender emotions. It was, and is, a world with which I am very familiar. John was searching for answers. He wanted to understand himself — his relationships with women — his life choices. Much of our time together during those momentous two weeks was spent working with John's Akashic Records to see his current situation through the eyes of his Soul. It was a new perspective for John, but it was one that, at that point in his life, he appreciated.

John ended up coming back to Minneapolis with me for a few days. As it happened, my friend and colleague who taught the Akashic Records class was offering a seminar in Minneapolis. As was common, whenever Dahna offered her class in the Twin Cities, I attended for support. I invited John to join me. To my surprise, he agreed. This was a dream come true. To have one of my family members step into my world was a pure delight. Again, a new chapter opened for us. For a while, we even considered working together using the Akashic Records to do business consults.

During John's visit, we also had time to meet a friend of mine for coffee.

Wes Hamilton is a well-known, master numerologist in the Midwest. One of the facets of numerology is that each letter in a person's name has a symbolic, numerical signature. The way the letters and numbers fall together provides a profile much like that of an astrological chart. We asked Wes to do a reading on our combined charts which identified the strengths, challenges, and spiritual purpose of our relationship. We thought it would be useful concerning the prospect of our going into business together. Getting readings from a variety of oracles – whether it's tarot, palmistry, Runes, or other sources – was, and is, a common practice for me. However, it was a unique experience for John.

Wes's reading provided invaluable information on how we might work together, but it also further solidified our kinship. After looking at the combined charts, Wes looked at us and said, "It's as if the two of you are twin personalities." Twin personalities are different than Twin Souls, as my husband Arthur and I are.

One relates to personality traits and the other relates to soul contracts, but Wes's reading added legitimacy to the comment his ex-girlfriend made about us being the male and female versions of each other. The synergy John and I felt in childhood was once again being validated. It was a gift that stimulated long conversations and deepened the talks we were having at that time. During one such conversation we, for the first time, talked about the distance that had come between us. I spoke openly about the rejection I felt from him and Keri.

He thoughtfully confessed, "The reason Keri didn't like you was because she was terrified of you. She was always afraid you would think she had a problem with drinking too much." She was right to feel that way: I had training as an addictions counselor as well as being a marriage and family therapist. I suspected before, but had confirmed that suspicion five years earlier when we had all met that weekend in Omaha to celebrate my birthday. But back then, I didn't care. It wasn't my problem. The family loved the fact that Keri was "so much fun." I had long ago let go of any investment in sharing my suspicion — let alone having it addressed.

However, hearing John say that made me wonder what my relationships to them could have been had Keri seen me as a resource instead of a threat. And I have to admit, it certainly felt good to have John acknowledge my suspicion. His admission re-established a closeness and openness between the two of us. But some part of me knew, even then, that the openness would be short-lived.

Less Vulnerability | |Renewed Distance

I was all too familiar with people being drawn to me when they were in crisis only to experience their closing down to me once the crisis had abated. That level of emotional vulnerability is not a place that most people live. So, I was not surprised when this eventually happened between John and me. As he became less vulnerable, he became less open. He never closed off again to me in the same way he had during that 20-year hiatus. But he did become less emotionally present. He shied away from my spiritual interests, and he could definitely be judgmental. I quickly learned it was important to be mindful when around him and to protect my heart.

As John was gradually shutting down to himself, and thus closing off to me, and more specifically, to my metaphysical interests, I was progressively becoming more involved in them. This created an even greater chasm between us in our beliefs and approaches to life. John had visited my world, but it was not a world in which he was going to live.

Learning about and applying metaphysical tenets to my life, and even in my work with others, became a priority. My experience with working with the Akashic Records, the records of one's Soul, became central to the foundation of my inner child/ Soul modality. I began to actively develop a method of working with others that took the thread of their inner child pain, wove it into their compulsions and addictions, and then braided those patterns into potential lessons of their Soul. I wrote a follow-up book to my *Inner Child Workbook,* entitled *Which Lifetime Is This Anyway?* The book was metaphysically based and introduced my newly- developed method of multidimensional healing. The professional circle with which I was involved consisted of Master practitioners such as Wes, but also psychics, mediums, astrologers, Shamans, medical intuitive healers, spiritual healers, and the new energy therapies of EMDR and EFT. I was even inspired to obtain advanced training in EFT, which is the self-administered form of acupressure. This direction in my life took me further away from those who were part of the mainstream. It took me further away from John.

JOHN'S LIFE TAKES A TURN FOR THE BETTER

Fortunately, John did settle back into himself when he met Jodi. Jodi was, and is, amazing. I said when I met her, and I have continued to say since I have known her, that there is no other woman I respect more. She has climbed the corporate ladder to some very impressive heights, and yet, has retained an open mind, a soft heart and an integrity that is beyond reproach. John and Jodi dated for several years and in 2008, decided to get married. I think Betty, Mom's best friend for over seventy years, perhaps said it best: "John has hit the mother lode!" They were a good match.

As a single woman, Jodi had adopted two girls from China. Alexandria and Samantha were still young, but she had made and executed this decision herself. John always wanted children. At their wedding reception, John boasted about how blessed he felt to not only be joining his life with Jodi, but to also be gaining two lovely daughters. He was elated. Six months later the adoption was official, and John was finally a father. He had the family he had always wanted.

Jodi was, and continues to be, close to her family, and every one of us benefitted from her becoming part of ours. I found this to be true when in 2009, Mom broke her hip again. This time John was not as available. I was working as a director in a Chemical Dependency and Recovery Treatment facility at the time and continued to live in Minnesota. Mom's rehabilitation was taking place in Nebraska, and by this time I had assumed, or perhaps *re*sumed, my role as Mom's caregiver. For six months, I traveled back and forth on extended weekends tending to her needs. It was exhausting. Every Sunday night I would pack things up and head back home.

Often, I would stop at John and Jodi's place in Omaha, which was halfway between Mom's home and mine. The stop made my drive doable. Every time I stopped, Jodi was there to greet me with a great big bear hug. We didn't have to talk. Her hug grounded me and helped me transition from Mom's life back to my own. I had great support from my siblings and childhood friends at that time, but Jodi's hugs were the most constant and consoling. I came to depend upon them.

Mom's hip healed, but she never fully recovered once she fell. She was 93 years old. The time came when it made more sense for me to quit my job, step in as Mom's primary in-home caregiver, and assist in her end-of-life transition. Mom died on August 26, 2009. Just as I had been the only one present when Dad died, I was again the only one present with Mom at the time of her passing. There is something very sacred about being with a person when they take their last breath. I truly felt it was an honor, and I knew what needed to be healed between us had been.

The next two months after Mom's death were spent sorting through her affairs, dividing her belongings, and each of us coming to terms with our loss. I was still living in her home, but each sibling came to offer their support. It gave us a chance to grieve together and sort through our respective feelings.

When John came to help out for a few days we talked a lot

about the past relationships between all of us and especially about the healing that needed to happen between Mom and me. "I knew, Cath, I was always Mom's *golden boy* ... that happened when I was the only one with her after Dad's breakdown. And I knew things never quite healed between you and Mom after your relationship to Walter. That's why in the last few years I stepped further and further back. I knew you had peace to make, and I wanted to be out of the way so that could happen."

His assessment was accurate. Those last five years of Mom's life *had* been healing for us. The months after I left my job to take care of her full time were perhaps four of the most rewarding months of my life. And he was right: if he had been around available, Mom would have kept me more at bay.

FAMILY LIFE CHANGES ONCE THE MATRIARCH PASSES ON

The death of the matriarch, especially if she is the center of the wheel, dramatically impacts the family dynamic. No longer pulled together for family holidays, Mom's surgery transfers from one facility to the next, her funeral, and the sorting through her affairs, we each drifted into our respective lives. The most significant change, however, was with John and Jodi. Employment opportunities prompted a move to Ohio. It was a big change for them and left a void for everyone who knew them.

My relationship with John, Jodi, and the girls, morphed into holiday and birthday calls, an exchange of presents at Christmas, which was done through the mail and an occasional phone call from John when he just wanted to "shoot the shit." We didn't see each other again until the spring of 2015. It had been six years since Mom's funeral. I needed to be in Chicago for two consecutive weekends. Chicago is a lot closer to Cleveland than

Minneapolis, so I decided it would be a good time to go visit John and his family.

That trip was the beginning of a new chapter for John and me. His calls became more frequent — our conversations more deliberate, often covering topics we were both facing, like getting older, staying in shape, and being positive. We shared information about books we had respectively read and even bought a few books on how to age gracefully that we simultaneously read and discussed. We joked about escorting each other through this stage of life in a positive way so we could *enjoy* old age instead of fearing it as Dad had.

In the fall of 2016, John called to tell me he had seen his cardiologist. He was scheduled for bypass surgery in late October. He minimized the risks, while playing it off as no big deal. As it turned out, when they operated, he ended up needing a *quadruple* bypass. He had been walking around with a heart attack just waiting to happen. Luckily, they caught it in time. He was in excellent shape — his recovery progressed positively — or so we thought.

In September 2017, I got food poisoning that lasted for over five weeks. It was horrible. I couldn't keep anything down but Annie's animal crackers and Coconut Bliss ice cream. It had been 15 years since I had eaten sugar in that fashion, and I seldom ate wheat. But in those five weeks, that's all I could keep down. I lost a ton of weight and felt weak. One morning John called. When he asked how I was doing, I began to rant and rave about how sick I had been and how weak I felt.

This was not a common conversation for us. John and I had always been the two in the family that took pride in staying physically fit. But when I finished my monologue, John chuckled and said, "Jesus, I could say the same damn thing. I was doing pretty well, but I just seem to have lost my *mojo.*" We joked and complained about our mutual lack of energy. Our paths were again merging, but this time more synergistically and collaboratively. We vowed to stay in better touch.

And we did, just not in the way we thought we would. On October 1, 2017, there was a turn of events and thirteen months later, John was dead.

Not only does Cathryn deeply touch on the quintessential family dynamics, she offers a journey to healing those wounds and expanding our potential in relationships, even after a person transitions. I couldn't stop reading this heart expanding book. A must read for those that have lost someone close.

Kim Eisen, Master of EFT 'Tapping' – Life Guidance Coach
www.LifeMasteryMethods.com

Your Thoughts and Comments:

_____

_____

_____

_____

_____

_____

_____

_____

_____

_____

_____

_____

_____

_____

_____

_____

_____

_____

_____

_____

CHAPTER FOUR:
JUST WHEN WE
THOUGHT IT WAS SAFE

THE BEGINNING OF THE END

I WOKE UP THAT morning in the same way I do most mornings, focused on making my first cup of coffee, and checking the emails and texts that had come in during the night. There was a family text from Jodi. "I just got to the emergency room. I think John has had a stroke. I'm waiting to hear what the doctor has to say now." The message sent chills down my back.

For several weeks we did not know what was happening. At first, he was on a ventilator. Then he was conscious but not very coherent. They continued to run tests. Jodi was fantastic at keeping each of us informed. John did progressively gain strength and became more and more cognizant.

Once he stabilized, I called Jodi to ask if it would be okay if I came to visit. She said, "Yes, that would be great. In fact," she went on, "just the other day John asked if it would be okay if you came ... because as he put it ... Cathy is really good in situations like this."

It was comforting and affirming to hear John had said that. And I didn't recognize it then, but in hindsight, it was as if John's Higher Self was sending out the signal to my Higher Self that it was time for me to come back into his life in a more conscious way. I had similar stirrings that called me back into Dad's life when he got close to death, and I knew when it was time for me to leave everything and go be with Mom in her end-of-life transition. I have intuitively known when some part of me was being called into service. My world may not be one in which my family members wish to live, but when one of them is in need, I am called back in … if not by them directly, then by their Higher Selves.

By the time I arrived, it had been determined that John had suffered an aneurysm. He was recovering nicely and was already back home — however, not for long. A few days after Thanksgiving, he was back in the hospital, and he wasn't gaining strength as quickly as they hoped. I visited a second time several weeks later. He was weak, but psychologically alert. I spent as much time at the hospital during that visit as I could. We hung out, watched CNN and movies, and periodically, just "shot the shit." But then there was this moment when everything shifted, and our conversations were never again the same.

THE REACTIVATION OF OUR SOUL AGREEMENT

We were walking the halls of the hospital intensive care unit when John paused, turned to me and confessed, "I've thought a lot about death in this last year, and I am okay with it if it happens. I think it will be kind of cool, like the next big adventure." There was a long pause. It was as if a judge had pounded the gavel calling to order a conversation that was destined to happen. There was a bench near the nurse's station. Without comment, we both sat down sensing this was the first of many conversations, such as this that we would be sharing.

We talked about our thoughts concerning death, life and the afterlife. At one point in the conversation, John chuckled and said, "Hell, Cath, half of the conversations I actually have now are with dead people. I don't see why I wouldn't do that same thing when it's me on the other side!" We both laughed and spoke even more candidly about our shared anticipation of not only the death experience, but also of the afterlife communication that could possibly occur.

Of course, we thought his death would be farther down the road. We didn't openly acknowledge that there may be another aneurysm hiding in the shadows of his brain. But on some level, we knew this was the case. Our spirits had reconnected — the contract our Souls had made long before we knew each other as brother and sister had been activated. But we didn't acknowledge this then. Hell, *I* didn't even recognize this then. Only now, over a year after his passing, can I look back and realize that this was exactly what took place. But at that time the journey we had agreed to take together was not in our conscious awareness. We were focused on the present moment and at that juncture, John did get better. He did return home.

LIFE RETURNS TO NORMAL, BUT NOT FOR LONG

The phone calls became more frequent, and John started relying on me again as he had in childhood. He'd call me to talk about his day, to ask what he should do about a certain ailment that I may have experienced, or to see if Arthur and I would be willing to transport the dog he wanted to get from Minneapolis to Cleveland. The *Soul agreement* may have been activated, but what we were aware of was that hope had been re-established, and the sister-brother bond had realigned.

There were many moments in those next several weeks when it seemed completely feasible there would be a different ending to this story. It seemed John had battled death and had won. Their family had made it through Christmas, had said goodbye to the challenges of 2017, and all were hopeful that 2018 would be a year of health and prosperity. The situation looked so promising that on February 7, together they had booked a family trip to the Bahamas for the upcoming spring break.

However, that hope was suddenly eclipsed with fear the very next morning when we received another phone call from Jodi. This one was even more heartbreaking. "John woke up today with a terrible headache. The paramedics just came. He's unconscious. I'm following the ambulance to the hospital." He'd had another aneurysm, but this one damaged the part of his brain that rendered him noncommunicative. He did not remember who he was or who Jodi and the girls were. The prognosis was guarded and unknown.

JOHN, ARE YOU THERE?

I was at home in Minneapolis. Again, I was unable to go to him right away, but I began to tune into his Higher Self every time I meditated. It was my way of praying for him. However, I also routinely checked in with my friend Darlene to verify that I was indeed contacting John's Higher Self.

Darlene, my intuitive friend, had been in my life since 1985. She had seen me through every major event since that time, from the publication of my book; my relationship with Walter and banishment from my family; through the deaths of my Dad, my pets, and Mom; to my remarriage, which involved the relocation from San Francisco to Minneapolis. She is not only a trusted friend and colleague, but one of the few individuals with whom I can confer regarding metaphysical matters. She confirmed that

John was teetering on whether to stay or go. It was again several weeks before I could make the arrangements to go visit him. But during that time, I made a daily effort to connect with his Soul even though his human self was still noncommunicative.

Shortly after his second aneurysm, before I went to visit him, I was invited to be a guest on a radio show with a well-known medium. As I said earlier, my life was becoming more and more entrenched in the metaphysical world, and this relationship was one that I had recently begun to develop. Once we were off the air, I briefly explained the situation and asked, "If my brother is noncommunicative and checked out much of the time, can I still communicate with his Soul?" She simply replied, "A Soul is a Soul is a Soul, and the Soul will *always* hear you."

When I was finally able to go to Cleveland, I was hesitant, reluctant, and unsure as to what I would encounter. As it turned out, the part of John's brain that held his past was still intact. Much to our surprise, when I walked into his hospital room the nurse turned to him and said, "John, do you know who this is?" Expressionless, he looked at me and nodded, "My sister."

It was a bittersweet moment. The fact that he recognized me was a good sign. The fact that he still did not recognize Jodi, Alexandria, now 17, and Samantha, now 15, was heartbreaking … so was the vacant stare he would get whenever we would try to contact him. He may have known I was his sister, but he wasn't able to sustain eye contact or have a conversation. The hospital staff advised us to ask him to blink if he understood something we said. With enough prompting, we could usually get a response.

There were moments, however, when I would lean into him and try to hold his stare. I was searching to see if I could draw him back into the physical realm. He would vacantly hold eye contact, but just when I thought I was making progress he would yawn and turn away. On one such occasion, Jodi was observing my attempts. When he turned away, she chuckled and said, "Just when you thought you were having a moment!" We both laughed, but I realized just how many moments like that she must have experienced. I could not even begin to imagine how heartbreaking this all was for her.

Nonetheless, I held onto the hope that some part of John was reachable. At one point I made another attempt. We were alone. Not quite sure if he could understand me or not, I stood up, leaned into him, and said, "John, are you there? Blink if you can hear me. Blink if you want me to continue to connect with you — Soul to Soul, on that higher plane." His response was downright comical. He started blinking incessantly. It was so obvious it made me laugh. It was so real that a part of me didn't believe it. Again, I had to call Darlene to confirm that what I had experienced had indeed occurred.

I returned home holding onto that moment of confirmation. He had said yes to me in the only way he knew how — present or not present. I held onto that as a sign that he was willing and able to connect in that other realm. It was quite satisfying for me, but there were few with whom I could share that excitement.

And I never lost sight of the fact that I was detached from the day-to-day loss that his family and friends were experiencing, as well as removed from the mundane needs that had to be met.

Jodi did a miraculous job of staying on top of things at the rehabilitation center. It took stamina and perseverance and by late spring, she had successfully nursed John back to a communicative state. By July, which was the next time I visited, he was still somewhat delusional and too weak to return home. But he was present, and his humor was back. There was a gleam in his eye. He knew who people were, could carry on a decent conversation and for the most part, it appeared as though his soul had *decided* to stay.

Jodi and the girls had to leave town for a couple of days. She didn't want John to be alone without having visitors, so she called and asked if I could come and stay. I cleared my schedule and went to spend time with John. My two godchildren, Lily and Thomas Allan, accompanied me. The four of us laughed and played *UNO!*. It felt as though I had my brother back. The edgy parts of him were essentially gone, at least with me. It appeared the part of his brain that had been damaged was that judgmental, condescending part. That made my time with him very pleasant. At one point John and I called our sister, Suzy. Unbeknown to me Lily videoed a few minutes of the phone call. Without knowing it, she had captured that "Taylor-humor" and gave us a priceless memory that later was a source of great comfort and joy.

Whatever disparity had come between us over the years was gone. It was like spending time with the baby brother I knew when we were young. However, I was forever mindful that this was not so for Jodi and the girls. They had lost a partner and a parent. Our two experiences could not have been more different, and I never lost sight of that fact.

FINALLY: A LIGHT AT THE END OF THE TUNNEL

When I returned home, I shifted my attention back to completing a professional training I had all but abandoned. I found it challenging. I'd been trying to complete the requirements for this training for a few months. It included recording 10 sessions that were then shared with my supervisor to demonstrate I had mastered the procedures sufficiently to warrant certification. The frustration had been monumental. Each time I tried to record the live sessions something would go wrong. Either the audio was off, or the video would fail to record a vital part of the demonstration. Each failed attempt required that I round up another new set of four to five people with whom I could demonstrate this new technique so that my readiness could be verified.

Ordinarily, I am very comfortable with videoing and demonstrating my expertise. But with this endeavor, time and time again my attempts were thwarted. With the last failed attempt, I pleaded with my supervisor to use a video of a previous session. Inside I just kept hearing myself say, "I just have to get to my brother." The minute I heard the words, "OK, you are certified," I clicked off Zoom and booked my flight to Cleveland.

This was late October 2018 and it appeared as though John was recovering nicely. It had been a long road, but he and his family had triumphed. There was now a lot of hope and expectation that John would return home. And it was all on account of Jodi — never has there been a more dedicated spouse than Jodi. She had managed John's care and navigated through doctor's appointments, red tape, and multiple calls involving insurance coverage. Each morning she would tend to the girls' needs, then on her way to work, stop at the hospital for an hour or so to make sure John had shaved, brushed his teeth, gotten his morning Diet Coke, and was dressed. After work she would pick up the girls, and they would again go to the hospital to visit. For seven months Jodi had done that — and after great effort to get John admitted to a more intensive care facility that would accelerate John's return home, she finally succeeded.

He was being admitted the very day I arrived. Jodi, in fact, was transporting him to the new facility as I was taking my Uber to their home. I called and asked how he was doing. It was the first time he had been in a vehicle other than an ambulance in over seven months. He chuckled and said, "We're having lunch at Taco Bell!" Then he jokingly quipped, "Hey, do you have your dog with you? I'm dying for a dog fix!"

Unfortunately, I had flown so I didn't have my dog with

me, but just him asking me that question was evidence that my brother was indeed, back. I had arrived too late to see him that night, but by the next morning, I could not wait to walk through that door. And even though I had visited John as many times as I could in that past year, there was something different about this trip. I felt a sense of urgency. My heart was beating fast. My belly was full of the kind of excitement a child has when getting ready to engage in something anticipated for a long time. I later told Jodi I felt like the sister who had run home from school to put calamine lotion on her little brother who was suffering from chickenpox. I had that same need to offer comfort and support.

I opened the front door. My attention was immediately drawn to my right where I saw the information desk.

"Good morning, Can I help you?" The nurse acknowledged me with little feeling and less eye contact than was warranted. "Hi. I'm here to visit John Taylor. I'm his sister. I believe he just arrived yesterday." "Yes", she replied. "He just finished lunch, and they have taken him back to his room to clean him up. I will let his Nurse know you are here. Please have a seat and she will bring him out to you." Again, I felt this sense of urgency. The restlessness had been building for months. And now, as I sat in the waiting room, I could barely contain myself. Finally, they wheeled John out. I breathed a huge sigh of relief. He looked up and greeted me with that "shit-eating grin" of his. My heart relaxed. We sat at the table and once again "shot the shit." And this time, there was more laughter.

There were times when we would chuckle as we did when we were kids. There were also more heart-felt conversations — deeper, more reflective conversations. At one point, he confided in me about feeling like he had messed things up with our niece one time when he had visited. He said, "I was just stupid." I knew about the situation. I agreed but withheld comment. He also casually stated that he had let the ball drop with our other niece, Cathy. "I really should have made more of an effort to keep in touch with her." Then, almost as an afterthought, he said, "Yeah, I'm ready to make peace. It doesn't make sense to hold onto things." His reflection was moving, but it was his next statement that meant the most to me. Without making direct eye contact with me, he said, "Yeah, I really mishandled that whole situation with Keri and you — but you know when you're married, you just kind of side with your spouse."

I was speechless. There were a thousand responses I could have given, and yet, not one of them was needed. The fact that this thought even formed in his mind was enough of an acknowledgment for me. Also, to her credit, Keri had long ago gotten into recovery and had established a sober lifestyle. I've been around the recovery world enough to know that holding onto something an alcoholic did during the height of active addiction is useless once the road to recovery has been found. But nonetheless, it was as if that old knot of tension was released.

My flight left early the next day. When I went to kiss him goodbye, I told him to hang in there. "You're doing a really good job. Just keep doing what they tell you to do and the next time I come you will be home." It was the first time in a year I left him with the confidence that a corner had been turned. Jodi's efforts had prevailed. He was positive, determined, and motivated to do what needed to be done so he could go home.

JUST WHEN YOU THOUGHT IT WAS SAFE ...

I arrived home just in time for my Condo's association's annual board meeting. When I met with the other board members one asked me how my brother was doing. I filled him in with some of the details and commented that I knew my brother was getting better when we played a game of *UNO!* (which I won, by the way). I shared that I had told John he owed me $100 because we had made a bet on the game that I won. I confessed I was pulling John's leg and laughed as I shared how John had paused for a moment, looked at me again with that infamous grin, and said, "No, I *know* that isn't true. My memory isn't *that* bad." I continued, "When I told my sister-in-law that story, she laughed and shook her head saying, 'Only a sister could get away with that one." The fact that we could joke about his memory impairment was a huge step.

The board meeting was boring. I was exhausted. I looked forward to climbing into my bed and back to some sense of normalcy. Instead, I returned to a phone call from Jodi sobbing, gulping for air, "John fell ... and suffered another aneurysm ... the doctor said ... he is not coming back from this one." There were no words to be said. There was only the silence of disbelief echoed by the sound of our shared tears.

Cathryn brings to light a deep awareness that we are so much more than human. She shares her vulnerability through an intimate look at her relationship with brother, John who has passed over. Their "memoir" offers a guide on how to deepen relationships with loved ones who are no longer in the physical plane as we get to witness a healing in their conscious relationship through playfulness, meditation, and encouragement of each other by working with their spirit beings of love and light.

Charlie Wagner, co-owner of Juut Salon's
Juut.com

Your Thoughts and Comments:

_____

_____

_____

_____

_____

_____

_____

_____

_____

_____

_____

_____

_____

_____

_____

_____

_____

_____

_____

_____

CHAPTER FIVE:
Endings are Beginnings Turned Backwards

The Beginning of The End

FIVE HOURS AFTER I boarded my plane to go home, John had tried to stand up on his own. We didn't know at first whether he had slipped and lost his balance, or if he had suffered another aneurysm. The details were irrelevant. The only words any of us were hearing at that moment were those that said, "John would not be coming back." By the time Jodi got to the hospital he was unconscious and on a ventilator. Two days later, Jodi and the girls stood by his bedside as they pulled the plug. Although he was unresponsive, he lasted another four days.

I found it curious that the period from John's fall to his actual death began with one of John's favorite holidays, Halloween. In many countries, October 31 marks the first day of the "Celebration of the Dead." It's a four-day holiday during which family and friends honor their deceased loved ones. It's not so much a gloomy or morbid occasion, but rather a festive and colorful holiday celebrating the lives of those who have passed on. Somehow being in the window of that holiday gave that six days a celebratory reverence. It was comforting to know that in many places on our planet, there were gatherings honoring those that were already on the other side.

I considered going to Cleveland to be with Jodi, but when I asked if she needed the support, she assured me she had the support she needed. Vita, a good family friend, was there, along with Jodi's sister and her Mom. I felt relieved. I was willing to be there for Jodi and the kids if they needed me, but my true feeling was that I would offer more support to John if I connected with him in the unseen. I spent as much time as I could during those six days in meditation. I felt close to John then and was supporting him in the most rewarding way I knew how. At 3:30 pm on November 6, 2018, John transcended his physical body and let go.

The moment I received the actual call that he had passed was surreal. I was at a school getting ready to register for an adult education yoga class. My phone rang. It was Jodi's number. The minute I saw the caller ID I came to an immediate stop, grabbed my heart, and burst into tears. I knew it was coming. I was ready for John to die. But that actual moment of finality surpassed my metaphysical perspective. Yet, just as stunning was the fact that it was immediately eclipsed by an undeniable sense of joy.

November 6 was also the day of the national election. John and I had discussed our respective feelings about President Trump and the upcoming election many times. I had to vote. I was on a mission to vote. As I walked in to get my ballot, a woman innocently asked, "How are you today?" Again, the whole situation felt unreal. Part of me wanted to exclaim with glee, "My brother just made his transition! It's so cool." For obvious reasons, I restrained. I don't care what part of the country you live in, or which circle you travel in, to say those words to a stranger thirty minutes after you find out your brother died would sound ridiculous. But what I did feel in those next few hours and days was just that.

I attribute this to the fact that I am an avid follower of Esther Hicks and *The Teachings of Abraham*. For those of you who might not be familiar with these teachings, according to Esther and Jerry Hicks, "Abraham" consists of a group of entities that are "interpreted" by Esther Hicks. Described as "a group consciousness from the non-physical dimension," the teachings consist of lessons about vibrational alignment with our Higher Self and the readily available relationship between the physical and non-physical worlds. Death is presented as a joyous return to our natural, non-physical state, which explains the ease with which I could feel so much joy. I have listened to or watched their videos on YouTube, and attended their gatherings having been inspired and directed. But not until John's passing did I realize how much their teachings had infiltrated my life and impacted my belief system. For the life of me, I could not *sustain* grief and sadness. I could feel it, but I couldn't hold it. I felt compassion and sorrow for Jodi and the girls. But *my* brief moments of sadness and grief were replaced with ecstasy and joy. I just kept hearing references to death I had paraphrased playing over and over again in my head.

There is no death. There is just a lifting out of the physical form and a return to your non-physical self. They are standing right next to you and if you want to connect with those who have crossed over all you have to do is align with your Higher Self, move beyond your sadness and grief, and expand to your highest vibrational frequency to experience resonance. But you need to expand to them. They cannot come to you. They cannot lower their vibration, only you can expand yours through your alignment with your Higher Self.

Even though I had played with this concept during John's illness, his actual death brought that experiment to a new level. I began to spend as much time in meditation as I could. I kept looking at this picture ... sensing and feeling my way around and within the progression from our human body to our spiritual one.

Whenever I elevated into my higher vibrational expression, I instantly sensed John's laughter — it felt like a vibrational force field of joy. There were no words exchanged, but there was his unyielding presence. Was it real or imagined? I had no clue. Yet, I felt no need to justify it one way or another. It made me feel close to John, and for that I was grateful, which was nice ... while it lasted.

THE AFTERMATH

Even though I had not gone to Cleveland during that last week of John's life, several days after his death, I was inspired to fly there for the first memorial. I knew Jodi was well supported, so I went more to be with my nephew, Sean, the one from California and my sister's son. Sean and I were close. We had been close when he was a child, and we continued to be close as he grew up. Sean had just turned 39, and he had been close to his Uncle John. Out of all the nieces and nephews, Sean was the one that had continued contact with him before and after he got sick. Sean had flown in to support Jodi, and I felt the need to go support him. We were the only two from John's side of the family to attend. It felt good to share this experience.

That first memorial was held at their country club. I agreed to be the greeter. I didn't know many of the people from that part of John's life. Yet, when I became immersed in the grief of everyone who came to pay their respects, I crashed into the human loss of my brother. I knew it was bound to happen. No matter how spiritual one is, the feelings of our human loss need to be addressed, otherwise we are just kidding ourselves. But man was it ever a jolt to drop into those feelings. It was so warm, expansive, and fuzzy to stay in that spiritual reality of John's passing. But every time I introduced myself as John's sister and heard the words, "I am sorry for your loss," the truth that my baby brother was gone became more real. I *knew* the spiritual connection was intact, but the physical loss of him was just as tangible and earth-shattering.

I remembered a workshop I had presented some years earlier. Kim Eisen, my friend, and co-presenter, offered a discussion about the exchange of energy that occurs when we become involved with others. She explained what happens when we physically part with loved ones — be it in response to their death, a divorce, or a mutual decision to separate. This is not a direct quote, but what I remember is that as a relationship between two people forms, there is an inter-dimensional, energetic merger that takes place and joins them together. Regardless of the reason, when the relationship ends, it takes time for that energetic entanglement to unravel and return certain previously co-mingled energies to them respectively. I can't do justice to the concept here, but I knew enough to draw comfort and understanding from her explanation during this part of the transition.

The way I personally experienced this was that I could simultaneously feel the vibrational *merger on a Soul level*, while at the same time be aware of the vibrational *attachment on the physical one*. There was great pain with the attachment. Being around his immediate family, his friends, and with Sean eased that pain. But I have come to realize that navigating between the physical nature of this world and the spiritual nature of the non-physical one is perhaps the greatest challenge of not only managing death, but also managing the trials and tribulations of simply being human.

THE LAST "ROAD TRIP" TO THE FINAL CELEBRATION

John was cremated. Transporting his ashes from Cleveland to Omaha where the second "Celebration of Life" was to take place became a challenge. Jodi didn't want to take the chance of transporting them by plane, so Sean and I became the official "ash couriers." The day after the first memorial we rented a car and began our last road trip with the three of us. We drove as far as Chicago where my husband met us for a concert. The second memorial was that next Saturday, so Sean spent the week in Minneapolis with Arthur and me — a week that was good for all three of us. We perched John's ashes on our fireplace mantle. It felt as though he was among us. And it was lovely to be in the safety of our home and the arms of my beloved. It grounded me as I emotionally prepared for the *last* official goodbye.

I did feel inspired to make one gesture. Part of me saying goodbye to John involved my desire to assist each of my family members in understanding his death. I promptly purchased a number of copies of Echo Bodine's book entitled, *What Happens When We Die* (New World Library, 2013). Echo is a beloved member of the Twin Cities spiritual community, but she is also a world-famous psychic, healer and best-selling author. For years Echo's *Center for Intuitive Living,* located in Minneapolis, provided a gathering place for classes and events servicing "newbies" to the metaphysical world, as well as those that are seasoned and like-minded. Gifting family members with her book was an invitation to expand and understand John's passing in a deeper way. Some read it. Others did not. But I at least felt I had done my job at nudging them in their expectations after John's physical ending.

"MOST OF THE TIME HE THOUGHT YOU WERE A KOOK"

Over 300 people showed up for the second "Celebration of Life." This one was much more heart-wrenching because it involved our childhood friends and all our extended family. Growing up in a small town means that you come from an environment in which everyone literally knows everyone. Everyone knew John and everyone knew the "Taylor family." Tales were told and memories were shared, first privately — and after a sufficient number of cocktails — publicly.

The first to take the microphone were John's lifelong buddies. Each shared a story that captured the longevity of their friendship. My brother, Tom, spoke about childhood pranks, and my sister, Suzy, shared a story about a family vacation. When I took the microphone, I shared what was pertinent for me at that moment — stories about the last year of John's life — about the conversations we'd had about death being the next big adventure.

I jokingly shared that story of when John turned to me on our hospital walkabout and said, "most of my conversations are with dead people." People laughed as I assured them he would most definitely be open to any conversations they may want to have with him.

In the spirit of that moment I handed the microphone to the next person. As I left the podium, I recalled this heart-warming experience I'd had right before John died at the same moment my eye caught a glimpse of one of John's longtime friends, who was also a family friend. He was familiar. I felt compelled to share it with him.

Somewhere in our conversation I turned to him and said, "You know I just remembered this really cool vision I had of John shortly before he died. I saw him standing in this circle of beings — some appeared to be Guardians and Angels and others seemed to be Loved Ones who had already died. It was so cool. They were all holding vigil for his earthly body, assisting him in letting go. And John was coming in and out of standing in the circle as well. Then at one point John looked over at me looking on — he got this big, shit-eating grin on his face — you know, that grin John always got when he was delighted about something, and said, '*Cath, this is so fucking cool.*'" I paused and took a deep breath. I hadn't remembered that story when I was standing at the podium, and it felt exhilarating to share it.

Unfortunately, he didn't share my sentiments. By this time, like many there, he'd had quite a few drinks. He took a deep breath, then slowly turned his head toward me and said, "You know, Cathy, in all honesty, I have to tell you that *most of the time John thought you were a real kook.*"

And there it was: a version of the truth that had seasoned the relationship between my brother and me since I received that letter the day I turned 30. No matter how many heartfelt exchanges shared, or amends made, the legacy of that division between John and me was always right there, hiding in the shadows, defining the dichotomy between who we were and who I always wanted us to be.

My automatic response was to quip back, "Yeah, everybody thinks I'm a kook until they are vulnerable or are getting ready to die." Now, to tell you the truth, I am not completely sure if I actually *said* that, or if I have just replayed that conversation so many times in my head that it has become cemented in my memory as the truth of that moment. But what is even more interesting to me is that every person to whom I have told that story, with the exception of my husband, laughed. I didn't. I was so open at that point and had experienced such heartwarming exchanges with John, before and after he died, that to have that version of our relationship thrown in my face took my breath away.

And even though I knew, in the end, John didn't feel that way, it solidified the truth that most of the time he did think I was a kook. And what was even more hurtful was acknowledging that for most of the life we shared, John had no idea how painful that had been for me. Yes, the sting of his comment took a long time to subside — it had thrown salt into a very tender wound. Yet, in hindsight, it is that very dichotomy that punctuates what happened between John and me, after his death, since his return to non-physical form, even more astounding.

CALLED TO DUTY FROM THE OTHER SIDE

After the celebration, I returned to Minnesota. I was emotionally and physically exhausted. However, what transpired over the next several weeks was a surprise even to me. My sleep was restless and through the night I felt the presence of John. Arthur told me I kept waking him up. He could never make out what I was saying, but it was obvious I was in discussion with someone. When I tuned in to ask my guidance what was going on, it was revealed that I was participating in John's *life review*.

The concept that our Soul goes through a life review once we leave our body at the time of death is well documented in books by such authors as Dannion Brinkley, Raymond Moody, Echo Bodine, and even Deepak Chopra. And, according to metaphysical studies and literature, when we sleep our Soul can, and does, extend beyond our physical body to experience a variety of spiritual encounters. Supposedly, the only difference between sleep and death is that the Soul sustains linkage to the physical body through what is referred to as "the silver cord." So, this phenomenon was not new to me. However, what was *new* to me was the idea of a loved one who is still part of the physical world *participating* in that life review. But that is exactly what was occurring between John and me.

And when I stepped back and reflected on what was happening it did make sense. I have dedicated my professional life as a family therapist to helping individuals resolve the pain of their past. It was a logical leap that John would call on me for that level of support given what had transpired in the last year. But what became alarming was the fact that I was beginning to feel *exploited* by John. I felt I was being called on to assist him in dealing with his unresolved issues while still feeling too stung by his death to be a willing participant. But the thought of having to set boundaries with a loved one on the other side — to actually say no to John regarding this situation — was another story until one morning when I woke up exhausted and exasperated. My dreams had been filled with activity. I sat down in my favorite chair and began weeping. Then I finally exclaimed, "John, I just can't do this right now. I love you, but you just have to resolve your unfinished business from this life on your own. I have my own set of challenges I have to settle."

I shut down.

I quit meditating.

I quit searching for John on the other side.

I needed a break from the intensity of walking between the two worlds.

I needed to come back to planet Earth and find a way to traverse through the many shades of grief that accompany the loss of a loved one.

THOSE SHADES OF GRIEF

There were myriad feelings I encountered over the next several weeks. At times I was able to hold onto the metaphysical tenets that there is no death, but more often than not, I traveled the other end of the spectrum. The emotions of the loss, the regrets and lost moments, unsaid words ... all filtered in and out of my conscious awareness. And the separation ... the separation of our physical selves ... it wasn't instant the moment John died. It was gradual and simultaneously comingled with a vibrational reconnection.

Then it began to shift. At one moment I would be enveloped in the pain of his absence. It was as if the essence of our physical relationship was being shredded. But then in the very next moment, that experience would give way to a more etheric connection. And once again I would sense him. hear him, and feel him near. Yet, I could only expand into that higher vibrational connection with John when I was willing to fully embrace the vibration of the physical loss of him. The grief zigzagged from elation and expansion, to sadness and contraction. And just as I had come to understand with the deaths of Mom and Dad, and even the deaths of my pets, I again experienced in a very visceral way, that there really is no separation: just that gradual, vibrational adjustment from what *was* to what *is*.

THE BEGINNING OF A NEW BEGINNING

The tumultuous emotions did begin to settle, but I found that navigating in the non-physical world when it was so personal was somewhat intimidating ... especially after I had pulled away from being such an involved support to John during his life review. About a month after John's passing, I had an opportunity to connect with Valerie, a friend of a friend who is a medium. A medium is a person who can essentially relay messages or communicate with a deceased loved one.

Although I often did this on behalf of my clients when we were accessing their Akashic Records, this was personal, and trusting what I was experiencing was challenging. It made sense to turn to someone who made her living from offering such readings. I asked if we could schedule a session. It was the level of confirmation I felt I needed.

We scheduled a phone appointment for the next day. At 7:00 pm sharp I dialed Valerie's number. I was full of anticipation mixed with a dash of apprehension, and I wasn't sure what to expect. As I mentioned, even though I had conducted sessions such as this in my own work, this was John — this was my brother, this was personal. It held an entirely different agenda.

Valerie answered the phone and graciously took command of the session.

"Okay. Let's just take a couple of minutes to take three nice, long, deep breaths to get grounded and to come fully into your body. Wiggle your toes. Just bring your attention to this moment." She then called in the Divine Energy, gave thanks for the information that was about to be revealed, and instructed me to state John's full name.

I complied. "John Alan Taylor."

She paused … "Ok, I sense John is here and is ready for you to go ahead with your questions." My first inquiry was general. I knew he had not been on that side for long. I was curious to hear her interpretation of his experience thus far. It was comforting to hear the response.

"He wants you to know that he has not gone away anywhere. He says that he often stands right next to you and that it *is* vibrational — that everything you've heard is true — that it was effortless, painless, a shifting of light." She chuckles, "He says he expected more … more drama, you know, more of a dramatic experience."

Hearing this made me smile. It felt so much like John.

"But he is also saying that it was surprisingly gentle, very gentle … and so he says he feels grateful for that. And that there's just so much love that he wishes to be able to communicate to people but that's been his difficulty — learning how to do that … everything is so new to him.

"Well, he says … it is … and it isn't. Time there isn't like it is here. It's not like what we think of it at all. And so, for him, it's been a time of learning how to express love to those that meant the most to him — to those that will continue to be important to him. And the power of love—he's been learning so much about the power of love."

John didn't usually talk about love like this. It made me

curious to ask how he was relating to specific people, like Jodi or his children, or even me.

"You know, he says he's working on all of those relationships, like tying up loose ends. He said this will go on for a while ... the healing. That's what he's been focused on ... where there has been pain or misunderstanding and bringing the power of love into that situation. And, whether that is registered on a conscious level or not with those individuals doesn't matter. It's happening on a very deep level with everyone, and he says it's profound: 'It is beyond anything I understood.' And, he says that he loves that he continues to grow, even now. And he's learning how to be able to hold expanded light ... he's saying that we keep so much away."

I interrupted her for a minute, "Wait, what was that? He what?" I wasn't quite sure what she had said, and it felt important.

"He says we keep so much away. We prevent ourselves from having so much that the universe is trying to give us, and that's the thing that he hopes to be able to help all of you with, is how to let the universe give more: more love, more support and more whatever it is you need".

I took a deep breath, and said, "Wow! That's pretty deep for John! I mean he just never talked like this before."

I continued, "Ok, Valerie I am curious about something. When I have done my own meditations and connected with John or have even been speaking with intuitive friends, I have been told and have sensed that the two of us would be working together, you know, in tandem — me here and him there. Is there anything he wants to say about that at this point or is it too early?"

"Ok," she replied, "Let me see how he responds." There was a moment of silence, and then again Valerie chuckled, and said, "Well he's smiling and says you don't need him to do the kind of work that you're going to be doing, but yes, it would be fun ... yeah," he says, "That would be a lot of fun!" Again, there was a pause. "But," Valerie continued, "that seems to be like a year or more away, in our time."

That was exciting to hear, and the timeframe made sense to me. I knew enough about transitions and adjustments to suspect that we both needed time to acclimate. I sensed we needed to learn new ways of connecting — and that neither of us had any idea how that would occur — or what steps would need to be taken to even begin to have this level of in-depth communication. But it felt comforting to hear that this was part of the bigger plan. The thought of John and I co-facilitating what I would call "multidimensional counseling" between those who are still in the physical world and those who have crossed over was indeed thrilling to even imagine.

The reading confirmed John was okay and that he was adapting to the vibration of the non-physical world. I asked if there was anything else he wanted me to know before we ended and his response was so sweet and genuine that it stayed with me for days.

Valerie concluded, "He says he wishes that you could feel all the love that's surrounding you ... and that there is much more to be shared between the two of you but you both need some time to adjust."

Having that connection with John put my mind at ease. I had the confirmation he was okay, and the promise there was much more to come for him and me. That was enough for then. He needed time in his world, and I needed time in my own. It was the beginning of December. There was the distraction of the holidays and a new year to begin. The timing was convenient. It is that time of year when reflection and redirection come naturally. Slowly life began to settle in and move forward without John in it – until one night several months later when he vividly appeared in a dream, and with that "shit-eating" grin of his he simply announced, "I'm back."

PART TWO:
"I'M BACK!"

THE QUINTESSENTIAL
LONG-DISTANCE RELATIONSHIP

Wow! A real page-turner! Warmly written from her heart, rather than her ego, Cathryn candidly discloses her life experiences and those of her brother, John, both separately and in relationship on this and the other side of the veil.

Jean Wallis, Psychic
(612) 874-1453 or jeanwallis@earthlink.net.

Your Thoughts and Comments:

_____

_____

_____

_____

_____

_____

_____

_____

_____

_____

_____

_____

_____

_____

_____

_____

_____

_____

_____

_____

CHAPTER SIX:
COMMUNICATIONS
FROM ALL SIDES

MY COMMITMENT TO JOHN

THE DREAM CAME a few months into the New Year. John's image swept in so dramatically that it woke me up, and in that half-asleep/half-awake state I heard him say with glee, "I'm back." My automatic response was, "Well, I'm not ... not yet! I need a few more weeks." I immediately sat up in my bed, shook my head, and exclaimed, "What the hell just happened?" I was filled with such a sense of anticipation and excitement ... the need to jumpstart my day with that first cup of coffee became a moot point!

And I *really* wasn't ready to jump into conscious dialogue with John right then. Granted, I had sensed John's spirit during his illness and his end-of-life transition, but this level of communication was different. I felt ill-equipped and in need of more preparation.

On March 3, I designed my plan for that preparation. Thirty-three is the day of the angels ... a good day to set the intention for our continued, expanded contact. I made my pledge to John and designed the protocols that would keep me spiritually, emotionally, and physically fit enough to show up for this level of communication.

3.3.2019: Intentions / Commitments / Regimens

John ... I have accessed the Akashic Record of our relationship as a way to come into alignment with each other. Hopefully, if I use this as a practice it will create a pathway for us to explore what we are to do together. I don't know what the rules or protocols are yet, but I reverently ask our respective Guardians, Teachers, Angels, and Souls for guidance.

I need help acclimating.

I need help knowing how to communicate with you.

I need guidance on how to discern exactly when I am communicating with YOU, John, versus when I am communicating with my own Higher Self and Guidance.

I need to know if that matters ... if there is even a difference. But beyond guidance, I am also just full of questions.

I was curious if I could connect with John anytime, or if there were certain parameters. I'd heard that communication is instantaneous in the spiritual world. So, I wanted direction on how to contact him. Did I have to make an appointment, or would he just be there if I called on him? And, I wondered what would be required of me in terms of my vibrational mix. I assumed it would work best if I connected with *my* Higher Self first and then asked to be connected to John's non- physical self, but I wasn't sure what the proper procedures were, and I wanted to be respectful.

I was grateful I could draw from the training I had established in 2003 when I ran my first marathon. I learned then how important structure was in successfully completing the desired goal. My *goal* was to learn how to communicate with John now that he was on the other side. That *desire* motivated me to regularly show up for my morning meditations that enabled me to elevate my vibrational frequency, which in turn, enabled me to attain and sustain emotional clarity. The workout regimen and food protocol I designed supported the sustenance needed.

On March 16, which would have been John's 65th birthday, I went into my morning meditation, opened our Akashic Records, and recorded our first two-way exchange. I wasn't disappointed. I felt his presence immediately.

OUR FIRST TWO-WAY CONVERSATION

I turned on my recorder and began to talk to John as if he were sitting in the chair right in front of me. I told him I wanted to trust what I was sensing from him. Even saying that little elicited great emotion. "I just want to trust, John, trust this is real." I took a deep breath, intending to wait for a reply. I hadn't even fully exhaled before I began to *feel* John's voice.

> *It IS real, Cath ... and I understand so much more now*
>
> *... there's not much we CAN do together right now. We both have a lot of adjustments to make, and we have just begun.*

Again, I was overwhelmed by emotion. It did feel real. We did feel connected. And the truth of that experience was beyond words. I told him happy birthday but went on to say that what I was really wanting to celebrate on this day was not so much *his* birth as much as the *birthing* of the new relationship between us. I had to pause for a moment to pull my thoughts together ... to again, remind myself that this WAS real. I wanted the communication so much, I was afraid my very attachment to wanting it so intensely would, in fact, energetically block it. But my fear didn't stop me from wanting to continue.

JOHN ... IS IT REALLY YOU?

When I shared this concern with John, I was caught by surprise at the depth of his response. It came so fast with no hesitation. I didn't have time to question it.

> *Ok, Cath, I don't know how to communicate with you vibrationally yet, either ... or you to me. But yes, I AM often standing right next to you. We do connect Soul to Soul. The more you connect with your Soul or Higher Self the closer we can be because I am already here. I am already in the non- physical. And you seem to act as a mouthpiece for OUR Higher Beings. It's not like you and I are going to do a lot right now. That comes later. You have more layers of your grief to go through, and I am still acclimating.*

> *We ARE going to be taught how to vibrationally respond and feel that resonance between us like we knew as brother and sister. And eventually, Cath, that connection is going to be so much broader than what we can even imagine now. We're just not quite ready yet.*

No one that knew John when he was alive would ever recognize those words as words that would come out of his mouth. Not only did John not talk like this, he didn't even *think* like this. But what was so convincing was that I could *feel* him.

There was no doubt in my mind that this was, indeed, an illuminated part of my brother speaking to me. I just had never experienced that level of consciousness from him before. It was refreshing. I was also amazed that he addressed my ambivalence to accepting this as real.

When I work with clients and am helping them connect with their loved ones there is not an ounce of doubt. I open the Akashic Records and hear their loved ones speak to them. It is genuine and real. But the difference between that experience and this experience with John which involved my believing it was John speaking to me was my attachment to WANTING it to be him. The more investment I had in wanting this to be true the more doubt I had to resolve.

Around this time I talked to a friend of mine who voiced the same experience. Carol Lowell is a well-known psychic and medium in the Minneapolis area and beyond. We were discussing this phenomenon on a radio show and she stated that she had similar doubts when it was her father who had passed. We both acknowledged it was different when dealing with someone we loved.

So part of me was elated, and part of me couldn't believe I was really feeling his presence this distinctly. But it was believable enough for me to continue the conversation.

John Speaks with Such Confidence

But I do know that we are definitely a part of each other's "Soul family," and we're both going to be learning about the multiple dimensions of consciousness as we move forward. I am going to be learning how to draw from your wisdom because you have been at this a lot longer than I have.

Where John went next was really a heart squeeze.

And what I have to say, Cath, is I am so proud of you ... of what you have done with your life. Now I can understand how difficult that was for you ... I mean in the context of our family. I understand the pain you went through with Keri coming into the family ... with my turning away from you ... with Mom and Dad turning on you. But you know, especially since my "life review," I understand more than ever, that before we are even born, we make those kinds of agreements. I know YOU know this ... you know that you agreed before birth that this lifetime would be one with a lot of challenges but also growth. So that was all part of it.

Now that level of insight I was not expecting. In some ways, it tickled me.

And of course, the acknowledgment of my challenge and difficulty with my family situation felt wonderful. But what was really astonishing to me was to hear him say ... "you agreed before birth that this lifetime would be one with a lot of challenges but also growth" with such authority and wisdom — a wisdom far beyond that which he exhibited as my brother in *this* lifetime. Experiencing John in this light was indeed uplifting. But then he continued with even more insight.

You began your spiritual evolution early in life. That was evident in how you showed up for Mom when she died. You weren't afraid of her death. You understood that end-of-life-transition ... for her and all of us. So, I can see now how you've been preparing all your life for what we are going to eventually be doing. Me ... not so much! I had to die to get on my journey, he said with a chuckle.

That comment left no doubt in my mind that I was speaking to the spirit of my brother. It was also intriguing to me that he referenced the experience I had with Mom during her end-of-life transition. That entire year had been full of life- advancing experiences.

It all started ten months earlier with the death of my 13-year-old canine friend named Kelly. Her death was as spiritually expanding for me as Dad's death had been. That experience with Kelly greatly enriched and augmented my ability to be present six months later with Mom during her end-of-life transition. Our story, which illustrates the methods I used to accomplish that task, is detailed in a book I wrote entitled, *Beyond Compassion: The Love that took them Home.*

And ... it IS true what John said. Those two death experiences were monumental. It was the first time I skillfully applied the many techniques I had learned (such as EFT/Tapping, a self-administered form of acupressure) and had developed (such as my inner child healing modality) to address such a gut- wrenching experience in my own life. The death of a pet or a loved one such as a parent, partner, or child, is supposed to be one of the most difficult experiences one can face. But my experience was expansive and uplifting.

Now, granted the circumstances were not tragic or sudden; but they were losses, nonetheless. They are losses that I can now look back on as tender and real. I *was* able to stay present during both transitions and because of that, my heart opened in a way I had never before experienced. John was right: I *had* been preparing for those transitions since early in life, and the same was true for what I was now experiencing with him. As I was pondering the divine order of each of these rather painful experiences, an interesting phenomenon took place.

THE EXCHANGE TAKES AN UNEXPECTED TURN

Suddenly I felt John step back and *my* Higher Self stepped forward. I could still feel John. He was still near. But my Higher Self became the dominant voice in the conversation. It was the first time I felt such a contrasting distinction between the vibrational signature of John and that of my Higher Self. When I sense John, I first feel him in my heart. It's a sensation of warmth that slowly expands as my heart feels inflated with love and light. But when my Higher Self emerges there are waves of energy that ripple through my body. It is as if my entire electro-magnetic field is being recalibrated, preparing me to experience a higher vibration of communication. When my Higher Self speaks, I pay attention. And that is exactly what she instructed me to do.

Listen ... listen carefully ... because this is important for you to understand. When you hold a vibration of love for an extended amount of time in one area of your life it increases your vibrational capacity to receive in every other area of your life. It positions you to receive all the Universe has to offer.

Your commitment and passion for staying connected vibrationally to your pet and your mother during their passing, and now to your brother, elevated and continues to elevate, your consciousness to expanded levels. As those expanded levels are achieved you will discover they, in turn, enable you to access and sustain a higher vibrational resonance with abundance and prosperity in your day-to-day life. Remember how your income increased right after you and your pet prepared for her transition?

For those five weeks before I assisted Kelly in her transition, my attention was focused on pure love and appreciation for her. I continued seeing clients, but my focus was definitely on the situation with her. And it is true: the next month I did experience a marked increase in my income even though I had not been thinking about money. My Higher Self continued ...

You witness this today in the profound empowerment you experience in response to the spiritual clearing, affirming, and intending you and your husband do daily.

Creating that force field around the two of you impacts every

area of your life together and sustains an energy field around your relationship that pulsates vibrationally. That vibration is what enables you to manifest things in your life together ... more money ... more love ... more compassion. This was one of the first messages your brother gave you. That vibration enables you to receive what the Universe offers.

I was reminded of what John said in the session with Valerie. Before we completed the reading, when I asked if there was anything else John wanted to say. This was the response:

"He says we keep so much away. We prevent ourselves from having so much that the Universe is trying to give us, and that's the thing that he hopes to be able to help all of you with, is how to let the Universe give more—more love—more support—more whatever it is you need."

My Higher Self was not only reminding me how to "receive" more from the Universe, she was also pointing out how Arthur and I were, in fact, supporting that very endeavor in our daily spiritual work together.

My reaction, however, was very odd. I initially expanded and felt a sense of pride and accomplishment ... but then, just as quickly, I collapsed into this uneasy feeling.

MY PUZZLING REACTION

I literally dissociated. Communication with my Higher Self — as well as John — immediately ceased. At first, I recognized this shift in energy as doubt, which just as quickly morphed into pure, unadulterated fear. It made no sense. I couldn't put my finger on what this fear represented. The message my Higher Self was relaying felt exciting. And I loved the acknowledgement of the direct impact Arthur's and my spiritual work together was having on our life. So, *what* was to fear about that?

I took a "moment of pause" and remembered the importance of *tuning in* and asking not *what* was the feeling about, but rather *who* inside was feeling it? I knew these feelings did not make sense to me in present time. However, I also knew, when there is a drop in feelings such as this, some younger part of me from my past is triggered. I also knew I needed to address this collapse before I could effectively re-engage in this first two-way conversation with my brother on his birthday.

As an inner child therapist, resistance such as this had become familiar.

Whenever an illuminated part of us expands to a new experience there is often a younger part that bumps into fear. The source of fear is always different, but the experience of fear is predictable. Most of us learned early in childhood that change was threatening. I had come to understand from my own inner work, and my work with others, that this fear was most often related to a perceived loss that needed to be resolved. I instinctively grabbed a pen and a piece of paper and began stream-of-consciousness journaling.

MY INNER CHILD NEEDS HELP

Accustomed to going into a meditation and doing this kind of inner dialogue I asked the proverbial inner child/inner adult question: "Ok, who inside is feeling this fear, and what do you need from me?" I sensed it was my inner five-year-old, and I waited for her to speak. Tentatively she said she was afraid of feeling so much sadness. "I don't want to let go. It was too hard to let go of Kelly and Mom. I don't want to have to feel the loss of my brother. I feel like I just got him back." I knew, instinctively, "she" was referring to the fact that John and I had experienced that renewed closeness before his death. If I, as the adult, expanded to a new relationship to him in the non-physical, it meant she had to confront a new level of his death in "her" world. She didn't yet know how to connect to him in the non-physical world. It hadn't occurred to me to show her. But once I made this connection I knew exactly how to proceed.

I took a moment to access my most loving and illuminated self. I knew from years of experience I couldn't intervene from that collapsed state. I had to step out of the deeper feelings of my inner child and access the evolved part of me who could respond. The first defining key to successful inner child work involves the ability to *separate* from the inner child's pain so an inner adult can *respond* by offering the comfort needed for him or her to feel safe.

WALKING MY INNER CHILD BACK TO SAFETY

This kind of healing happens in the imagination. It is a proven fact that the mind does not know the difference between what is real and what is imagined. "What we can conceive, we can achieve." And, in inner child work this is *achieved* through the *interaction* between an empowered, nurturing self that, again, can *respond* to the fragile self and make him or her feel safe. I took a moment to envision my most empowering, nurturing, and confident self. Once I had fully embodied her, I *imagined* I knelt in front of my inner child. I proceeded to reassure this younger self I knew how to navigate through these feelings of this loss and that I could teach her how to connect to her brother in a new way.

I paused for a moment to get a sense of how she was responding. I had her attention, but she was not yet convinced I would keep her safe and protect her from the fear and despair. I continued to reassure her. Even though the conversation between my inner child and illuminated adult self was comforting, my inner child needed to be reassured the love between John and her (or us) was not gone.

EMBODYING THE VIBRATION OF OUR BROTHER/ SISTER LOVE

To meet the need of this inner child I had to retrieve a memory when John and I *were* connected when he was still here, in this dimension. I recalled when Mom died, and even when Kelly was gone, it brought me great comfort to look at pictures of moments in my life with each of them when that pure, unadulterated feeling of love was present. My mind began jumping through different experiences with John that had been captured in a photograph. Suddenly it landed on a picture that Jodi had just sent me. It was a picture taken of John hugging me at the end of my first marathon. I began rummaging through my desk to find it. I knew once I had that photo I could share it with my inner child and assure her that anytime we missed John, we could look at that picture, return to that feeling of love, and we would be automatically connected to him. And there it was: that smile, that hug. This photo captured the love between John and me. This was the vibrational connection I was looking for — the connection that would help my inner child understand there truly was no loss. That feeling of love kept our connection alive. Looking at this picture repeatedly, recalling that moment, those feelings, and sharing that experience with my inner child enabled us to bridge her fear and doubt to my faith, excitement, and love.

And there it was: that smile, that hug. This photo captured the love between John and me. This was the vibrational connection I was looking for — the connection that would help my inner child understand there truly was no loss.

This toggling between my inner child and my adult self — between my human self (or ego) and my Higher Self – became a constant theme in this expansion. Either the part of me that had a hard time letting go would emerge, or the doubter part of me that feared this was not real would surface. I had to stay aware of those collapses and converse with those more fragile parts. When I combined these conversations with the technique of EFT energy tapping, (again, a self-administered form of acupressure) a longer-lasting resolution occurred.

We all have parts of us that are not as evolved as the more illuminated, adult part. This dichotomy becomes evident anytime we are growing and expanding into new levels of consciousness, into new vibrational frequencies. Something I always say in my work with others is that when we expand and evolve and "bring in more light and awareness," we simultaneously bring more light to our shadow selves ... those parts of us who hold fear and despair. *I call these fragile selves our inner children.* The illuminated part of each of us is that adult part that has lived through empowering and expanding experiences. Our adult self is made up of the culmination of all the successes of our challenges. We, in our adult consciousness, not only are proof that we survived what the inner child experienced, we can now share what we mastered to succeed. We can draw from what we learned and now help those more fragile parts come into harmony.

My collapse was in direct response to what John and I were trying to create. My desire to grow pulled "her" out of her comfort zone. My Higher Self's message about how this directly impacted every other area of my life was intimidating for my inner child. It was my responsibility to resolve this discomfort before I could continue. But once that was done, I was able to return to my conversation with John, and when I did, he assured me he had been on the sidelines observing this whole interaction. When I asked if there was anything we needed to talk about right now, he smiled, almost as if he were impatiently waiting for me to finish so he could get back to what he was saying.

Well, yes, just one last thing ... there really is no "life after life" as you know it. There is a substance to the being I am, but the energy is different. My vibration is different. I still have some of the personality I had, and some of the traits I had ... some of my jokester self. And there are a lot of people up here that I know and hang out with just like I did down there. But I'm also in school. I've done my life review and there were some parts I'm not proud of. But we can get into that another time ... there is so much more we need to talk about ... but we have time. We have all the time in the world, Cath.

I would've liked to have heard more, but the communication slowly faded. For the next month or so I continued to check in with John, and when I did, I felt his definite presence, sometimes stronger than others. But I came to understand that the quality of the connection between us was governed by my openness at that moment, not by John. There was something about the communication with John I was just not trusting. It seemed like a good time to seek outside validation.

A possibility presented itself one day when I received a phone call from a friend named Carmel. Her mother had just died. She continued to share that she had been so distraught about the loss she had contacted Samantha, a well-known medium in her area. She wanted to see if her mother was okay and to ask if there were any messages her mother wanted to bring to her. Carmel's experience with Samantha was informative and helpful. As we talked further my interest in setting up an appointment for myself peaked. It felt like an opportunity to get validation for what I was experiencing. I contacted Samantha to set up an appointment for myself. She lives in Ireland, so we scheduled a Zoom call.

As the day approached, I felt more and more excited. What came through in this reading was exactly the shot in the arm I needed – and as you will see, it confirmed my experience and communication with John were indeed real!

So beautiful to read. I am genuinely so happy you get the answers you need to hear. It is also wonderful for me to experience. I am and will always be in ahh of spirit world.

Samantha Doyle, Medium
hi@samanthadoyleemotions.com

Your Thoughts and Comments:

_____

_____

_____

_____

_____

_____

_____

_____

_____

_____

_____

_____

_____

_____

_____

_____

_____

_____

_____

_____

CHAPTER SEVEN:
THE GAME-CHANGER: A READING WITH A MEDIUM: PART 1

A GIFT FROM A FRIEND

AT THE DESIGNATED time, I sent Samantha the Zoom invite, and within seconds we were connected. We exchanged hellos, and then Samantha explained that sometimes she used tarot cards for the reading, but at other times the client could simply ask the questions he or she wanted answered. I opted to begin with the questions that I had.

She confirmed my primary goal was to connect with John ... then added if John is indeed willing to come through.

Well, I muscle test and ask if he's here, and there's definitely a connection. I sensed energy around the house just about an hour beforehand, and I felt someone even in the car ride to the store with me just enjoying the scenery. So, it's funny that way. Do you want to start and just ask some questions just to make sure that you know you're connected with your brother?

I decided to begin by asking what kind of communication John wanted with me. But right away, John had another agenda.

ABOUT HIS HEALTH AND HIS TRANSITION

Okay. He first wants to speak about the health issues when he was passing and the medication that was given to him then.

I agreed that starting there made a lot of sense because I had wondered if the medication interfered with a clear transition. I thought that might have been why it took him so long to die because his brain didn't know what to do. It felt as though he was ready, but had a hard time getting in sync with his body so it could let go.

Samantha confirmed this was the case.

The feeling that he's giving me was that the medication was more of a hindrance than a help, as in "it caused me more problems than it helped me. It felt like I was just getting an injection and injection, and stuff was just going into my body while my entire being was screaming, 'No!!!'"

Okay, now he's saying that even though you weren't there, as in your physical presence, your energy was always around. I feel that you gave him healing energy ... you helped ease the transition, those are the words coming to me ... and you helped him surrender and release a lot of the emotions that he carried. I feel, whether you know it or not, whether it was your presence or your words, you helped him to heal a lot of his human life ... if that makes sense to you. It helped him to let go ... and I also feel that he's showing me, "I had multiple problems in my body ... it wasn't just one thing. It was one thing that led to another." He says, "I felt pain, but it was mostly in my torso and my arms."

That clarification was helpful. The next topic I was interested in was how John wanted us to move forward. I had some hint about that from our communication, but again, I was looking for confirmation.

WHAT DOES HE WANT TO DO TOGETHER NOW?

As you were speaking, I did muscle test this to be true, yes, 100% true. And I know. Cathryn, you already know this

... I know you know in your Soul and your heart he is with you. He is now telling me that you have a nickname for him, it makes him laugh, and I see a red t-shirt as well, I'm just giving you everything he's showing me ... he's just showing me like a nickname, and a red t-shirt.

I laughed and told Samantha that my nickname for him was "dipshit!" I would often address him like that when he would call ... or I would call him ... "Hey, Dipshit ... what are you doing?" Samantha and I both laughed, then she continued.

No wonder he's laughing.... Okay, he says please don't stop saying that to him. Please, keep it real. Keep it like there's just a veil ... and I know, Cathryn, I'm telling you stuff you already know ... but he just keeps saying, "It's just a veil. I'm sitting right beside you." He's giving me images ... you're sitting down to have a bite to eat, a bite to eat is in front of him and he's going through the motions ... when you're working, he is connecting on a stronger level than any other time. He says, that's because that is when your vibration is the most clear.

People feel that feeling that they're in the presence of their loved ones, and he says, he is there, and he is watching. Whether you speak or not, he's feeling you. There's a heart-to-heart connection here. It's not just Soul to Soul ... it's a much bigger bond. He's saying that he's speaking through you already, and he's given you some ideas about how to follow up with your work but you're questioning it. He says that when you get that way, and you're frazzled, you need to bring it back in.

Okay, I'm going to say it to you as I hear it, "just anchor those feet into the fucking ground ... just stay with me. You're my only link. Anchor your feet into the ground because I need you to fucking keep clear ...."

Samantha paused mid-sentence and chuckled.

He is using some coarse language here, I don't usually talk like this, but he says that when you're frazzled and you feel your grief emerging, he will pull his energy back a bit so he doesn't overwhelm you ... so he can keep that connection with you. And he's saying that there are others he can't contact ... you're his link to here. "You're the strongest link I have. Anchor your feet to the fucking ground so I can stay clear with you, and don't frazzle out on me. Stay with me." So, he says he's around everyone, but your connection is the strongest. There are two other people, as well, that he's trying to connect with, but messages are blocked at the moment ... but it is just a matter of time and he's got all the time in the world.

Samantha then asked me if I have any other specific questions I want to ask. I explained that I don't really have a list, but instead, I described an experience when Arthur and I were at a movie, and I just felt John sit down in the chair next to me and say, "Yup.

This is exactly the kind of movie I want to see." When I told her that, she laughed, and I continued.

"So, I do have moments like that. Or I'll have moments when I'll do something stupid or comical, and I'll hear him make some wisecrack. I still miss his sense of humor a lot."

Yes, yes. He says, "Don't change the way we've spoken to each other. Stay real. Call me a dipshit, you know, keep it real. Keep me alive in your mind, your heart, and Soul

... just like I'm here. It's only a veil away. You know I'm there. When you feel that surge of tears and overwhelm, and I feel too close, you can ask me to step back a tiny bit. But I'm not leaving you, and if you ever feel that you just need time, I respect you and will give you all the time that you need, but..."

Samantha's voice dropped off for a minute ... as if she was trying to listen.

Ok, so now he's showing me a wooden plaque ... a wooden plaque that he has given you or you gave to him. It's a message on a wooden plaque, but there's a twist and a joke to it.

I paused for a moment. I couldn't think of anything that related to that right then, but two weeks later it hit me.

SOMETIMES IT TAKES AWHILE

I was putzing around in my living room and all of a sudden, I remembered that for Christmas one year, back in the early 1970s, I had given each of my siblings a wooden plaque with a picture shellacked on it. I had taken pictures of my brother and sister with their spouses and used those for each of their gifts. But John wasn't married. The *unique* picture I could think of using for him was this photograph of him when he played the role of Harvey, the invisible rabbit, in his junior class play. If you've never seen the play, which was later made into a movie starring Jimmy Stewart, Harvey was an invisible rabbit that only Jimmy Stewart's character could see.

I was awestruck. I realized that was what John was trying to tell me during this reading! Not only did it verify it was John coming through to Samantha ... but it was also a very clever way for him to suggest that he would be my *invisible* partner.

I became obsessed with finding a copy of that picture. I certainly had no idea what had happened to the plaque. Come to think of it I don't recall my brother's and sister's plaques being displayed anywhere either, so evidently, it was not one of my better gifts for any of them! But I do distinctly remember that John was not thrilled with my choice of *his* picture.

I spent the next several weeks feverishly looking through the family photos to see if I could retrieve it. Then, one day, I was driving down the freeway and I suddenly thought of Carol, one of my high school friends. She's married to Steve, one of John's high school buddies. I quickly texted Carol and asked if Steve still had a copy of their junior high school yearbook.

Ten minutes later she sent me a text ... with the photo! Steve happened to keep his yearbooks in a basket next to his easy chair. Carol wrote that sometimes he just likes to pull them out and look at them.

In ten minutes, I had the picture on my phone. I couldn't believe it ... what confirmation!

I called Carol immediately to tell her the story. When we hung up, I heard John say, "I did that!" I had a smile on my face for the rest of the drive home. That one incident "sealed the deal" for me to believe this was John coming through in Samantha's reading. But the benefits of this reading didn't stop there. As the reading continued more pearls were revealed. One that was especially significant for me was John's response to a question that held a great deal of interest for me.

AND WHAT ABOUT OUR WORKING TOGETHER ...

"... I mean from his dimension *and* mine." I shared how I had recently been working with a woman whose daughter had committed suicide. I opened the Akashic Records of both mother and daughter, and then did what I would call *multidimensional family work*. I brought in the Higher Self of the daughter so she

119

could help her mother better understand why she felt she had to take her own life. It's very profound to work that way and with that depth. That's an example of what I'm hoping John and I will be doing a little bit more together down the road."

He says he definitely wants to work with you. And in some ways, he already is. "There are so many ideas I have now because I can see things I couldn't see before." And, it's like he says, "I want to lift the blinkers. You KNOW I'm here. You KNOW I'm right here."

He says all you have to do is sit in your favorite chair, and when you've let go of your day and let go of all your talk, and when you're in that space, that's when he can connect to you.

Okay, there was the John I knew: pushy, demanding, and forthright. It warmed my heart to feel his personality coming through so strongly! I was still curious about us working together, but the reading took a detour.

In *I Think I Like You Better ... Dead*, Cathryn Taylor has given us compelling and persuasive testimony that the spirits are real, and that physical death is not the end of spiritual life.

Timothy Cope, author, adventurer, and shamanic practitioner
https://rattledrum.com/

Your Thoughts and Comments:

CHAPTER EIGHT:
THE GAME-CHANGER:
A READING WITH A
MEDIUM: PART 2

BUT WAIT ... THERE'S AN EVEN BIGGER PICTURE

Ok, now he's showing me conversations you would have had where you would have spoken about passing over, and what life would be like on the other side. Does that make any sense to you? I feel like he's saying, "We've had these conversations. We have been curious together, but it is more than we could ever imagine."

"So, was that helpful, that he and I had those talks?" I asked.

Yes, she says, laughing. He's so colorful with his language. I just keep feeling like I want to curse! Ok, so now he's saying, "It's fucking amazing. This is more than you could ever imagine." I'm asking him to show me, but he's saying, "I can give you a feeling, but it's a snippet of a feeling." Okay, now he's making me aware, though, that when you do allow yourself to stop the mind from telling you the connection is wrong … he says, "I'm there with you. I'm giving you images, giving you the feeling. I can only share so much with you."

Okay, he says he has full respect that you're grieving

… and he has full respect that you have your life, your commitments, and everything else that you want to do. But he is there, linking, ready to connect. But if anything is blocking you it's your grief and your doubt.

I commented that I knew I had doubts. I never had doubts with Mom or Dad when they died. But this seemed so much more real with John, and we were so verbal about our beliefs. Yet, I just needed to make sure I wasn't kidding myself.

No, no, you're not, and that's exactly what he's giving me here. "It's not the same as Mom and Dad. Our link is stronger. You're going to feel more, and that's why you're questioning yourself. Please don't question yourself. You know, make notes. Write things down.

You don't have to share the experiences you're having with me with everybody because not everyone is going to get it … not everyone will. Just allow yourself time to trust yourself … trust our link. Write it down if you feel you need to express it, but not everyone is going to understand when you say, 'I connected with my dead brother.' They're going to just laugh."

That statement made *me* laugh. "Well, I'm used to that. In fact," I said with a bit of sarcasm, "if he remembers correctly, he was *one of those* that laughed."

He says he knows that, but he sees things differently now, and he wants you to trust that. Again, I feel what he's just saying is that you have this, you believe it, you understand it, but then you start to pull it apart, and you start to question it. And he says, "What the fuck are you doing? Why are you questioning this when you know all of these feelings are real? You're pulling things apart. You're trying to diminish it. You're not going to get away with it." He says, "I'm not allowing you to get away with it. I am going to keep coming faster, stronger, harder, until you start trusting the fact that I am here with you. I am just a guide. I am going to guide you to keep going."

He says, "You have so much more to do. We've had this conversation. It's important to help others push through, push past the veil. You need to open up people's minds so they can see more ... see that relationships don't have to end here."

You've had these conversations with him, and this is what you do in your work with others, and to that, he says, "Keep pushing. Stay focused. You're touching more Souls on this planet, and more people than you can imagine. Those that you work with, that you connect with ... you ripple through their families ... you ripple through their friends. You're not just working with those people one-to-one. You touch their whole community."

Samantha paused, then continued ... *I don't know if you've stood on a stage with a microphone and had conver-sations like this with people ... but I feel I want to stick a microphone in your hands. I feel that is where he wants you to be. I think he wants you on a stage. He wants you to get this because there are more and more Souls out there that need to hear this. They need to know. They're reaching out, but they just don't know which way to go.*

Samantha paused again. *"When you throw that stone into the pond, and you have that one person that you've got in your class or a one-to-one session, then that branches out to all the people, and it's like networking, but they (meaning John and my Guardians and guides) say there are more and more coming and you better be ready." He's like, "I'm ready. You better get ready. This is bigger than you can imagine, and it is coming from the other side".* She laughed. *I feel I'm putting you on a, you know, when they cart the drinks into a bar on a wheelbarrow ... what is it called? Oh, he's showing it to me in my mind, so it's where they would carry the cartons of drink into the bar with the two wheels ...*

"Yes, yes," I told her. "I know what you're talking about ... a dolly cart."

Yes, that's it, that's what I see. I feel like I want to scoop you up and run you out onto the stage like that ... don't hold back. You have this audience. He says, "Just get out there and say it, and speak it. Don't hold back. I'm expecting more and more from you." That's exactly what he's saying.

"Hmmm." I paused to take that in… "Well, it seems he's still as pushy as ever!" We both laughed.

THE CONNECTION BETWEEN OUR SOULS

Okay. Do you have another question?

"Yes, I have a question about the exact nature of the connection between our Souls, and what we are to each other, and about the other times, we've been together. I was told at one point by a numerologist that we were twin personalities. And when I was at his memorial, I had somebody ask if we were twins."

Samantha chuckled then became serious again. *Yes, for two lifetimes you've had the twin energy ... two times ... two lifetimes the twin energy. He says, "Not in this particular lifetime, but we're thick as thieves." She laughs. He even had me write that down ... so he says you would have been that close when you were younger ... you were thick as thieves. Did he use that expression?*

"Thick as thieves ...," I wondered aloud. "He may have said that a lot. That wouldn't be outside of the realm of possibilities. And yes, we were close, but then there was a time in this lifetime when he turned away from me."

Okay, but I feel as you were just finishing that sentence, he was telling me it was when he was rejecting himself ... rejecting his true self.

"Yes, I think one of the things that I was most sad about after he died was the lost moments that we could have had that we didn't have," I said.

Samantha started chuckling, and her reaction felt a little odd, but it inspired me to inquire: "What's he's saying?" I could feel he made some wisecrack. "He's funny, isn't he?"

Samantha laughed again and then she continued emphatically. *"My God, wait until she gets to this side and sees how many lifetimes we've had together. Those moments are fragments, tiny dots. They are, you know, tiny."*

I laughed as well. *"You've got to remember where I'm at."* *He's like a little kid with a new toy. He's sitting there with this attitude again: Let it go ... get on board!*

This sounded so much like John. But I had to admit it gave me a warm feeling to experience his humor and pushiness again.

And he's saying, "Wait until she sees all the lifetimes which are coming. The two of us have had so many lifetimes together where we stumbled, but we've had many magical moments. Our connection this time around was ...

Samantha paused, and continued: *I want to say what*

*he is showing me ... It's like you had this telepathic energy.
You knew things. You could finish each other's sentences. You*

*knew how you felt ... you knew what was right at the time
of conversations.*

Samantha laughed. *Okay, he said, and I challenged her.*

With tongue in cheek, I reply, "Well, that's a *nice* way of
putting it." I then wanted to turn the focus back to what I need
to do next.

So, How Should I Connect to Him Now?

When I told Samantha that I wanted to know more about
what we do from here she asked for clarification on what I was
doing now. I explained that sometimes I played my meditation
tape to clear my mind and then just asked to come into communication with him. But I went on to describe times when I'm idle
– like driving or just doing something mundane – and I can feel
connected to him then as well.

*Yes, yes, That's exactly what I feel he's saying ... it's like as
soon as you step back, it's the typical and mundane in this life
... like when you're chopping or peeling vegetables, or filling
the dishwasher, or driving in the car, you're going into a
different mental state ... those are the moments when he can
connect. They are the moments he can drop in and give you
the reminders ... the memories ... the new ideas. I feel like he's
saying to me that he's given you two really strong ideas since
his passing, and you're dismissing them.*

"Hmmm ... big ideas ... like for my work?"

*Yes, it's for your work. It's for you. It's for all the people
that you want to help and the people that you work with.*

It's two really strong ones. He's given them to you, and it was during those moments where you were on your own.

I explained further, "Interesting. Well, that's what I am hoping to perfect more and more with us, is that kind of communication where I feel like I have a partner working with me. I mean, that's what I'm hoping our relationship could be, one where he's a very active agent in my work ... and not only with what I bring through in my meditations but also my sessions with others, you know? I work a lot with people who are trying to make peace with loved ones that have already passed. And, again, my vision is that he can work with the loved one on that side while I'm working with the person still in body."

Yes. He's getting me to write down the words "he's your ambassador." He is working beside you. He is aware of what you do, and he says if you ever doubt yourself once more about your connection, about the message you give to the person who is sitting in front of you, he is going to give you such a thump.

"He's going to do what?"

Samantha chuckled: *He's going to give you either a thump or a jab in the arm or something, the next time you doubt yourself. So, he says you better be ready because he is going to step in. No more doubts, my God, it's like you go, go, go and then you doubt. You go, go, go and then you doubt. He's there to help, and again he's saying, "I have your back ... I'm your ambassador."*

Hearing Samantha say that was so validating. It affirmed that our connection was real. And God it was comforting to think of John as my Ambassador. It not only fortified our continued connection but gave me a sense of that true partnership I had really longed for all of my life. To think that could now exist with John was a heart squeeze beyond measure. It kept me smiling for days.

ABOUT WRITING MY BOOKS

He now wants to talk about your writing... the way that you've written your books, I've seen it in your e-mails, but I want to tell you from his side ... he sees not only one, but he gives me two, two more books. So I'm to tell you, one first, and then a second one. There are already words put to paper and you've stopped it.

Astonished, I said, "Yes, there is one that's half-started that I haven't finished on the four stages of recovery. I'm an addictions counselor, so expanding the perception of recovery for our multiple addictions is a huge passion for me.

But, I've also had the vision of a book about John and me ... called something like, *Travels with my Brother*. Well, that sounds kind of dorky as I hear myself say it, but you know what I mean ... a book about the interactions we're having on all levels."

He says, "There are other ones that you'd like to tweak, but there are two more that you are to write ... one is about this journey of your continued connection. So, start putting the pen to paper ... both about how you're feeling and about the process that you're going through because your words on paper are going to help others do the same.

I wanted to make sure I understood what he was saying. "So, he wants me to sit down and just let him write through me. That's what he's asking?

Yes, but it will be a two-way connection ... like you'll

be writing, but you can talk to him. You can ask what he thinks. Then it will be truer. He has me putting my two fingers together ... my two fingers are side by side, so you'll be interacting together.

Ok, this was good. I was waiting for this confirmation, and I was almost done with what I needed to finish for my work, what I needed to develop that got delayed because of all that went on before he died. So now what I wanted to do regularly was to just sit in conversation with him and talk.

"So, he's suggesting we have a meeting regularly. I mean, I want to hang out with him too, but I also want to sit and *feel* him there at the table with me as we determine what we want to bring through together. Does it help for me to open our Akashic Records together? That's usually how I *officially* connect with him ... Higher Self to Higher Self, or I guess it is my Higher Self or my non-physical self, and now his non-physical self," I asked.

Yes. He gives me a definite yes! Yes, there will be moments when you call him in the way you call him in, and he will know that it's work time. It's different when you're in the car or you're walking or whatever you do. He's very aware. And as he said, he will suppress his funny side. He won't lose it, but he'll suppress it because he has a lot to share. And you know this, Cathryn, Samantha said emphatically, *I know you know this.*

He's saying, "She knows ... she knows we have that." You're not just connected casually; your whole being is connected. You are not just checking in with a loved one to make sure he is okay after death. My God, he's given you tons of evidence that he is more than okay. And what I keep feeling is that he's saying, "Are you ready for this? This is a whole new relationship for us?"

I knew I *wasn't* ready yet. I wanted to be ready, but I wasn't. I had proposals and workshops I had to develop, and I had to be patient with myself because the truth was that I wasn't quite there yet. *But* I knew I was *getting ready to be ready* as they say in the Teachings of Abraham. And right then, that had to be enough.

The Amazing Call from Our Nephew, Sean

What happened next was absolutely mind-boggling. I was getting ready to meet Sean in New York the following week. I wanted to ask John if he had any message for Sean. As Samantha and I were talking about our meeting my cell phone rang. "Oh my God, Samantha, Sean is calling me *right now*! I swear to God!" Samantha asks me if I want to answer.

I accept his call. "Sean, you won't fricking believe this, but I am right in the middle of a conversation with Samantha. She's a medium, and we are talking to John *and* we were just talking about how you and I are going to be meeting in New York in a few weeks. I swear to God!" Without hesitation Sean simply says, "Oh, cool!" We all laughed.

I got the bright idea to invite Sean to say hello. I put him on speaker phone and Samantha explained that she was speaking on behalf of John and that he was telling her to say hello. It all felt quite magical. We talked a bit back and forth and then I told Sean I would call him back when we were done.

Samantha and I couldn't believe what just happened. We talked a little bit about Sean's and my upcoming trip. I mentioned that I wanted to open all our records when we were together in New York.

John says that would be great ... he's telling me that he orchestrated all of this. He's getting a great kick out of it.

WRAP-UP QUESTIONS

So, I think John wants to move back to you now. Do you have any other questions?

I added, "Well, let's see, I can't think of specific questions, but I'm definitely ready to bring my focus back to my business expanding after all of this new training, and I think John and I can be partners in that.

Yes. Okay, you just have to tell him. He shows me traffic lights ... they're turning green. When you're ready to go, he's ready. He won't push you. It will be just pure teamwork. It's not even guidance. It will be teamwork, Cathryn. Normally you're receiving help from your Guides. Keep doing that, even though you've always done that. But I just keep putting the two fingers together. It's teamwork.

I asked, "Is that why I feel such a strong twin-ship with him? I feel that we're holding that twin-like vibration even though I'm still in my body."

That's the word, you just said it. It is the vibration.

Your vibration is different than most, but it always has been. You have always maintained a higher vibration. For your whole life, you were, I want to say the word "different."

It didn't take much for me to agree with that ...

Your whole life ...

"Yes, my beliefs were never really understood ...but John and

I did have a great last year, and even though he was suffering, he and I connected a lot in the last year," I pondered aloud.

This inspired me to ask about something I had often wondered about ever since John had passed.

"I always felt John was waiting for me to come that last visit because of some of the things he said to me on that trip, but also because it was only five hours after I left that he had his last aneurysm. I always felt as though I had gotten there just in time. Was that true?" I asked.

Yes. I see him watching the clock. Yes.

"Yes, I felt so much inner tension to just get to see him."

Okay, so I really have to confirm this before we end because he wants you to know that you did have an impact. Whether you were there or not, your energy served a purpose for him. But definitely, he was holding on for you, definitely!

He's wanting to close off here. I'm still going to say it how he said it, "Put pen to paper, but you do it your way, okay? But no matter how you do it ... just record notes." It will just come through and just sit with it, just allow him to show you different things. And you better be ready", he says, "Because I'm going to push you out of your comfort zone."

We both laughed.

You know, and again, the next time you doubt yourself there will be a jab. Okay, so John wants me to tell you whether he shows it to you or not, secretly he has such high admiration for you even if he didn't show it.

When I heard Samantha say that it was if all the times John

thought I was a kook just began to dissolve. Truly, there was such a healing in those words.

And even as I write them here, I still choke up. That feeling persists. It was (and is) as if every insult, and dig, and hurtful thing John ever said to me, or about me ... every rejection or judgment ... each incident was encased like an ice cube in a tray. And as Samantha spoke those words each cube of hurt began to melt and dissolve.

Wow! I thought to myself ... I got the message, John. ... then I say to Samantha, "Alright, Samantha, I'm sure that I'll be in contact with you again.'

I'd love that. It was wonderful to speak to you and a pleasure to be with your brother, John, and Sean coming through on the phone. How wonderful!

"And for him to be able to say hi to John. That's going to strengthen his belief," I said.

Yes. Well, I think when you were asking for signs you got one there and then.

I thanked Samantha and assured her I would be in touch again. I was ready to jump into this exchange with both feet. I was ecstatic about the prospect of our post-life communication. So, it didn't make sense that my enthusiasm came to a screeching halt. But it did.

It happened about three days after our session. And I struggled with that fact a great deal. But try as I may, there was a part of me that had shut down to this whole endeavor. I opened my Akashic Records and asked to be given insight and direction regarding this block. Finally, I was able to get some clarity.

In my mind's eye, I saw this younger version of myself, the

one that was in college and was waiting for her brother to walk through that door. She didn't want her brother to be dead. She was still waiting for him to walk into that student lounge and save her. Even entertaining the idea threw that part of me into such a state of grief it was almost unbearable.

If I wasn't an inner child expert I probably wouldn't have had the first clue as to how to even deal with feelings such as these. I don't think I would've even known enough to figure out that it was a younger part of me.

But it was. And I battled with her grief for several weeks. When I met Sean in New York the opportunity for me to open all our Akashic Records together presented itself. I got a taste of what it would feel like for John and me to really work together from both sides of the veil. That college girl within me finally softened. She began to see that her brother had finally come to rescue her, *to be* with her. His Ambassadorship was the key!

The door to that level of communication opened and from then on it was quite common to engage in conversations with John, either casually or officially. This became evident one day when I was walking around the trail at Cedar Lake near my home. Often, I would pick up my husband after work, and together we would go to the lake. He would swim his two miles, and I would walk mine. On this particular day, I suddenly felt John walking right along my side eager to converse. I had the same startled response I'd with the dream – except this time … I was ready.

PART THREE:
"FROM BROTHER TO AMBASSADOR TO PARTNER!"

I've known Cathryn as a fearless explorer of consciousness and personal empowerment for many years. So, I was struck by her doubt and uncertainty when she first told me about this journey she felt called to embark upon. I'm so glad she said 'yes' — because the book you hold in your hands is a unique and courageous invitation to hope, love, and redemption. It will change the way you look at life, family and what happens after we die.

DK Brainard, Master Astrologist and Shaman
https://dkbrainard.com/

YOUR THOUGHTS AND COMMENTS:

_____

_____

_____

_____

_____

_____

_____

_____

_____

_____

_____

_____

_____

_____

_____

_____

_____

_____

_____

_____

CHAPTER NINE:
WALKS AND TALKS WITH …
MY BROTHER/AMBASSADOR?

THE MAGICAL AND ENTERTAINING WALKS

THE NEXT SIX months were truly magical and entertaining. John was ever-present. The more I kept him real, the more real he was. We bantered back and forth as we did as kids, and he was right there ready with a wisecrack every time I did something that warranted one! And I gave him plenty of material…

Even though I'm incredibly competent in most areas of my life … (Okay, John's rolling his eyes at me right now … but really that's true …) but … I do have this "Lucille Ball" part of me that perpetually finds myself in somewhat comical (and sometimes, not so comical) situations. (He's vigorously shaking his head yes,) Fortunately, my siblings and I inherited this innate ability to laugh at ourselves … mostly from Mom. Dad enjoyed a good joke, especially before his nervous breakdown. But Mom – she loved laughing at herself. In fact, back in the day, when Mom was not disowning me, we often found ourselves in what we would call a "Lucy and Ethel" moment.

For those of you who do not know this reference, Lucy and Ethel were two of the four main characters from the early '50s sitcom *I Love Lucy*. Lucy and her sidekick, Ethel, were forever finding themselves in a series of mishaps that left the audience doubled over with laughter. My antics are a product of being preoccupied with so many details in my head that I fail to pay attention to what I'm doing in the moment. Unfortunately, this can be an ongoing occurrence, resulting in a continuous series of absent-minded adventures that to this day provide ample material for humorous exchanges between my husband and me. But now John had joined the chorus, and it was an addition that I thoroughly enjoyed.

At the other end of this humorous scale is the edge of criticism – the capacity to deliver harsh, piercing sarcasm that I call "The Taylor Edge." It was that "Taylor Edge" that was so hurtful in my relationship to John, but it was also that edge that softened after his severe aneurysm. I once even commented to a friend that it was as though John's series of brain bleeds destroyed that critical part of his brain and the Taylor humor had re-emerged, front and center. This was great for me as his sister. I didn't need that executive part of John's brain to enable him to be my co-parent or father. It is delightful now that he is in spirit form that this jokester aspect of his personality is intact.

And ever since the experience of locating that picture of Harvey and John supposedly instigating the timely call from Sean during Samantha's reading, John was taking credit for every good and inspiring instance in my life. After each, I'd hear John say proudly, "I did that!" And then chuckle.

Finally, one day I quipped back, "Yeah, yeah, I know, my life was rudderless until you died!" And then, there I was, belly-laughing in the middle of my kitchen with no one else in the room. I'm sure, had anyone seen me, I would have appeared quite mad. But it became truly delightful. I'd feel him shake his head at all my shenanigans. We'd both laugh and then I'd say something sarcastic ... like, "Jesus, don't you have anything better to do than 'haunt' me?" Bantering back and forth like this kept him alive in my head ... to the point where sometimes I'd briefly wonder about my own sanity. And I did periodically feel a little like Jimmy Stewart in *Harvey*. Was I perhaps going over the edge? Was this real, or was I just trying to keep John alive? Yet, time and time again I would get confirmation, in a thousand ways, that this *was* real.

But it was the more serious exchanges that elevated our relationship to that otherworldly dimension. When we were just walking and talking around the lake, or when I would go into meditation and purposely expand my consciousness to meet him at his new vibrational signature, his sage-like awareness was spellbinding. Those were the insightful times that fostered our continued growth, and it was then that I began to understand what he truly meant when he said he was my ambassador.

And it's not as though he was talking about anything that hasn't been said. No, the novelty was that we were having these conversations *at all* ... and that these conversations weren't hypothetical as they had been when he was "here." Now, John was sharing real experiences ... experiences he was having from the other side. His tone would change ever so slightly. His insights were profound ... his wisdom ... far beyond what he exhibited when here. These conversations ... left me wanting more.

For instance, since the reading with Samantha, I'd been inquisitive about what he meant when he said I was his *only* portal. Did that mean that the only way he could continue to experience things here, in this dimension, was through the vibrational resonance with me? Or could he actually "drop into" a baseball game, whether I was there or not? And more importantly, I wondered when I was conducting a session, or even a workshop, could he energetically be there *because* of our connection ... or did I have to call him in with intention? With all these questions swimming around in my mind, I decided one day to just ask him.

"YOU'RE MY ONLY PORTAL"

Well, I know that whatever you do, I CAN experience because of my connection to you. So, yes, that's exactly what I meant when I said you're my portal ... my strongest connection. You're the most open to believing I still exist. Your willingness makes it easier for me to continue to relate to you ... especially when you're CONSCIOUS of bringing me into an experience. I don't know how long they'll have us do this, but I do know there are specific things you and I are being "prepared" to do. I'm just not sure what those are yet.

But what we're doing now ... talking like we are right now ... this is how you keep me alive. When you relate to me like I'm real you keep that energetic bond vibrating. We're learning how to bridge that gap between the two worlds. That's why I said, "keep it real ... keep me alive ... joke with me ... talk to me ... call me dipshit ...that all keeps me real. That all bridges the gap."

We won't always have to be so "aware" of our connection. You'll get to a place where you take our continued relationship for granted ... then it won't have to be so forced. But right now, it's like flexing a new muscle. So, I'm not backing off ... I'm not leaving you. The intensity between us is needed ... it's too important. I'm actually closer to you right now, Cath, than I've ever been in terms of understanding you. It's interesting ... it's interesting to see how vulnerable and strong you are at the same time. That's a unique quality. I really do wish I would've taken more advantage of who you are.

I liked how John was taking command of these conversations. The next noteworthy conversation came a few days later. I asked John to explain more thoroughly the best way we *could* connect. I kept feeling like I had to do hours and hours of meditating before I could expand enough to connect with him. But he assured me, in a rather "cute" manner, this wasn't the case.

"NOT THAT MUCH HIGHER"

You're making this way more difficult than it is. Yes, energetically, I'm now at a different vibration than I was, but because of our incredible heart connection, the easiest way to connect is for you to simply 'pretend' I'm there ... right beside you. Get over feeling you must 'adjust' to a higher vibration. I'm just not "that much higher" than you are, he says with that million-dollar grin. *You've spent much of your adult life raising your vibration. I can finally keep up with you!*

With that statement, we both laughed. Then he got serious again and continued.

But I CAN see things clearer now than I could when I was there. I was pretty blocked. And I do need to say to you that when I crossed over there were a lot of a-ha moments, pearls of wisdom I could see from our talks that I couldn't see before. Even though it took me until the time of my death to see the value of those explanations of what to expect, they did accumulate and provided the stepping-stones I needed to get to the other side. You did that for Mom, and even for Dad, when they died. You showed all of us the way to get from there to here.

His tone then again changed ... it got softer ... more deliberate.

Cath, you do see beyond what most others see. That's why so many don't see who you truly are. You ARE between the two worlds of the psychological and the metaphysical ... and that must be hard for you because you can never find your "tribe." That longing you talk about has to do with that ... you don't belong to either of those worlds. One fears you and the other dismisses you. It's lonely. And I hope to help with that. I'm enthused about being your Ambassador, and I have a lot more to say, but there will be plenty of time for all of that. For now, just know you really are not alone. Think of it this way ... anytime you think of me ... I think of you — we're telepathically connected, and when you keep me real and you keep me alive, I'm there. So no, you're not making anything up. This IS real ... but God, I'll be glad when you get over that damn doubt!

We both laughed, but I still had so many more questions. I wanted to hear more about the telepathic connection we had, and I wondered how he could be with me in these experiences, and yet, be participating in what was happening over there simultaneously? But the connection suddenly faded out. It happened like that sometimes, and I never understood why. Was it me, or was it him? It was as if the "internet connection" just failed. The next time we talked I wanted to pick up where we left off. I wanted to understand more clearly how all of this worked.

WE'RE BRIDGING THAT GAP

Ok, so how DOES this work? Well, how I understand our connection is that there really is no place and time here. I mean I really can show up whenever you are open, no matter what I'm doing, because everything is truly multidimensional. I can be in more than one place at a time ... so no matter what I'm doing here, when I sense your consciousness calling to me, I can tune in to you in an instant.

But it's not like I'm always hovering. There are times when I do come to you ... and sometimes you sense me and sometimes you don't. But whenever you call on me, I can be there. I'm not limited by physical barriers anymore. It's actually kind of cool.

Now, again, the reason I can so easily anchor into you is that you are such a receptive portal. Literally, whatever you are doing ... when you invite me in ... I can vibrationally experience it. But I do respect your boundaries. Plus, I see things vibrationally. I'm not invading your private moments. You don't have to worry about me seeing things you don't want me to see. That's not what this is about. Pull the curtain, and I'm gone!

BUT ... the strongest connection we do have is when you're working. When you're counseling others, you're in alignment with your Higher Self ... and then I can be right there next to you. The resonance is incredible ... especially when you are present and consciously inviting me in ... you're the most receptive then.

Part of what my Guides are preparing me for is to be better at linking you to those that would benefit from your work. But they're also working on our relationship and training us to vibrationally work in tandem. We're a long way from doing that effectively, but I'm told that's where we're heading. That's the main purpose of my being your Ambassador ... of our continued relationship. It's not just for sport! He says, with a chuckle.

You have such a wealth of information, Cath. So again, I'll be aligning more and more with you so I can see that those who need your work find you – that's part of our contract. And, ultimately, I will work alongside your Higher Self ... not instead of your Higher Self ... but as additional support to your Higher Self.

But for now, what you and I are doing is figuring out how I can speak through you – how we can bridge that gap between the two worlds. But it WILL take us some time to flow with this in a way you can document. That's why, right now, it feels somewhat cumbersome because you're learning how to articulate what you hear. You WILL get better at taking this for granted. But right now, it IS an effort. Right now, you forget that I'm here. Right now, you forget that I'm so available.

THE PROGRESSIVE ALIGNMENT AND REALIGNMENT

I was beginning to understand "bridging that gap" meant that John and I were constantly adjusting to what I began to refer to as our "progressive alignment." Now that he was on the other side, HIS vibration had elevated enough so we could truly communicate. As he said, he could now "keep up with me." HIS non-physical consciousness now matched the elevated consciousness I had acquired through all my years of spiritual study. I had been preparing for this relationship for much of my life. The *veil* between us was thinner than most because our Souls had pre-planned them to be.

This is not always the case. As the Teachings of Abraham explains, most humans don't continue a relationship with a loved one once he or she has died because they don't expect to. But it doesn't mean it's not possible, and even sometimes, as with John and me, prearranged. I knew from past experiences there was no separation. Even though there were times I doubted it, I still had a part of me that knew this to be true.

But I was also beginning to appreciate that there was a process to all this progression. It wasn't immediate. It was gradual. I found it fascinating that after John's passing it took him time to distance from his human experience. This seemed to enable our otherworldly relationship to "evolve". His "human" personality was still evident enough for me to recognize his spiritual essence as being that of my brother ... and there was enough of my elevated consciousness available to him so we could connect, and bridge that gap, even though we were now on opposite sides of the veil. Furthermore, it made sense to me that as we both became more comfortable with his physical absence, and adaptive to the change in the dimensional connection, we'd be able to more effectively align on a higher plane with a collaborative, non-physical vibration. In other words, the transition from physical to non-physical was *progressive,* not automatic. I had never realized this.

But I still wanted more clarity, so I opened my Akashic Records. My Guidance further explained that as the deceased one acclimates to the other side their vibrational frequency changes. They step further away from the traits of their earthly personality. But, again, as my Guides put it, this happens gradually.

"The essence of the deceased loved one is still identifiable, but the human needs to be able to follow the alterations of the vibrational signature if the two are going to bridge that gap and remain connected. Often this is not the case, and it is experienced as though your loved ones have gone away because you do not know how to "read" their new, vibrational signature. The loved one becomes "less of who they were" as they expand to their ethereal body. The resonance shifts from being physical to being energetic ... from being identified through the five bodily senses to eventually being experienced through the vibration of the heart."

This explanation matched how I experienced John's presence. I always felt him first through an energy in my heart that then began to intensify. So that seemed to be the trick. If we were going to grow "together", we needed to learn how to continually realign and adjust to the progressive, expanded, vibrational frequencies. But it was becoming more evident that we ... meaning those on both sides ... human and spirit alike ... can't do this when either one remains attached to the old, earthly form of the relationship.

I suspected, from my background, that the antidote for this dilemma had to do with our ability to grieve each stage of a multi-dimensional relationship such as this. But I didn't realize this happened on both sides. We needed, however, to first find ways to navigate through the ebb and flow of letting go and expanding ... letting go and expanding. John needed to get better at trans-mitting information, and I needed to learn how to translate what I heard.

MAKING USE OF MY VOCABULARY

I was beginning to understand that as John and I went through this transition, it was my familiarity with his vibrational signature that was the fuel for this communication. I felt comfortable with that level of conversation because I could easily *translate* his vibration into what I knew of him as my brother. I "heard" his sense of humor, I "heard" and "experienced" the laughter and that felt real to me. John was talking through me. I'd fill myself up with the vibration of what I knew as John and then could *feel* our conversation like streams of thought that I translated into my own words. That's why what I "heard" from him so often sounded like my verbiage *BECAUSE IT WAS*. I was using my language to interpret what he was saying, and what he was saying was now taking our relationship to the next level. What we were accomplishing was successfully "bridging the gap."

I found this to be so interesting. I'd always been the one that was on the leading edge with the two of us, and now my vibration was following his lead. It was a little disconcerting. But I just kept hearing my Guidance say that I had to keep it simple. It was safe to follow his lead. They continually cautioned me to not complicate things ... to just keep it simple. They explained we'd be helping readers expand their expectations so they could begin to entertain the possibility of relating to their loved ones that have died. But then they said, *"Just keep it simple, but know that even this will change."*

Wait ... what does that mean ... "but know that even this will change?" However, just as I was processing these thoughts in my own mind, my Guidance receded, and John jumped back into the conversation to add his two cents.

> *Cath, there are so many on this side of the veil that are excited to contribute to what we're going to be writing about ... some of them you know ... well, you at least know OF them. But I will be bringing them into your awareness as consultants. They're excited, too, because it's rare for someone to be as open as you to their continued inspiration. They are*

scholars that have been influential in THEIR respective areas of YOUR expertise.

See, Cath, this is an example of how I'll act as your Ambassador ... there IS a direct line between you and me. That's why the relationship between us is just as important for my Soul development as yours. It's a cooperative, pre-agreed upon endeavor. Right now, we're perfecting our ability to bridge that gap between the two worlds. And we can do that because we're heart-connected and because of the familiarity and trust that strengthens our connection in a powerful way.

But it's all about bridging that gap. Once we have learned how to do that there will be a whole new adventure. But for now, it's about bridging that gap. I'll be continuing to drop in as needed, but you're definitely on the right track. We're using what you have already developed to build this bridge. It's built on the need for people to understand the inner child steps, the stages of grief, all the modules you've already created for expansion in the human realm. The ability to progress in THIS transition is being built on what you've already created. But we've got a good stretch ahead of us.

"Okay," I responded, "I get all that ... I understand it ... but John, what did they mean ... 'even this will all change?'" To which John simply replied, *I don't know either. I guess we'll see when we get there together. Right now, we just need to worry about bridging the gap.*

Cathryn's words are insightful, inspirational, and full of the wisdom of greater knowledge that stretches the understanding of what really is our total experience. Her work is daring and willing to look beyond.

Darlene Turner, Intuitive Healer and Acupressurist

YOUR THOUGHTS AND COMMENTS:

_____

_____

_____

_____

_____

_____

_____

_____

_____

_____

_____

_____

_____

_____

_____

_____

_____

_____

_____

_____

CHAPTER TEN:
TOGETHER: WE BRIDGE THE GAP

GRIEF FROM BOTH SIDES OF THE VEIL

THIS NEXT DISCUSSION John and I had was particularly timely and definitely was evidence that we had indeed *bridged the gap*! I never realized until I offered a workshop on grief that grief was something those on the other side had to address as well. It certainly makes sense … I had just never considered it. John seized the opportunity to show me this one day when I was getting ready to offer my workshop on grief, which I periodically do when the timing seems relevant. And it is almost always relevant on Memorial Day weekend.

It's common for me to offer workshops that correlate with certain American holidays. On Mother's Day, I offer workshops about healing the "Mother Wound"; on the 4th of July, I offer workshops about independence. It was Memorial Day 2019 … the ideal time to offer one on grief. Half of the world, or at least the states, would be grieving that day. I knew I was. And it seems when I need to process through a layer of my own grief, I'm often inspired to offer such a workshop. It *is* true: we "teach what we need to learn!"

I found the grief associated with this unfolding quite interesting … the constant letting go of the feelings related to my physical world as I expanded to the more etheric world where John could be found. I couldn't achieve one without letting go of the other, and often this resulted in a tug-of-war between these two parts of me. It made me even *more* curious about the veil that exists between the two worlds. I was getting accustomed to calling in John's energy when I worked. I did so the day of this workshop, and definitely felt his presence all day long. But when we spoke the following day, I found his comments intriguing.

> *You did a genuinely nice job yesterday with the Grief Workshop. I loved watching you work. There was great interest, by the way, on this side because most of us are still earth-connected due to our emotional regrets. Many on this side gathered around me because my connection to you made it easier for them to experience the workshop as well.*
>
> *That's the first time I experienced your work on the process of grief … but what I'm learning is that this is what OUR continued growth on this side of the veil is all about. Yes, we're in spirit form, but letting go of our earthly body and the emotions that are associated with it, is a gradual progression. And you and I agree that we cannot progress if we have that palatable energy … or as many refer to it, karma … that gets stored in the etheric body. It gets stored as different colors of Light and those colors represent different vibrational frequencies.*
>
> *So, it's not like we die, and poof, we're emotion-free, as some would suggest. At least not for those that I'm around. But what else is interesting, Cath, is that what I have been shown now is that this vibration of emotion is what each Soul uses to choose the "hue" or color of emotion the personality will be operating under for its next lifetime.*

I loved hearing these comments from John. It WAS beginning to feel as though he was operating on that "Ambassador" level. I knew he had attended the workshop because I *felt* his presence. But the idea that others could attend as well was highly curious. It made me wonder if those that attended were in any way connected to the participants in the workshop itself. But when I asked John about this, he said that was not necessarily the case. These attendees from the other side were attending because of their own agendas around the emotions of grief and letting go. It made me wonder, "In what way?" When I posed that question to John, he suggested I get clarification from my Guidance who knew much more about such matters than he did. But to my surprise, their response went in an entirely new direction.

THE VIBRATIONAL RESONANCE AT THE VEIL

"This is what we need you to understand. The veil is very thin, and it IS just a matter of vibrational resonance. Humans have to allow their consciousness to go to a higher frequency to match the vibration of their deceased one. It's not that their deceased one "visits" them. It's that the human expands his or her vibration and becomes receptive to ALIGNING with the loved one. But this requires their willingness to grieve, to feel their loss, and move on to a new form of the relationship. Most humans find this difficult.

That's why so much connection is made in the dream state because a higher vibration is more easily attained. But even the dream state can be convoluted by the human psyche. So often what appears in dreams is metaphoric. The mind does not always know how to embrace the information. This is where meditation becomes necessary.

If people really want to connect with their loved ones, they need to train their consciousness to get into a higher vibration."

ABOUT MEDITATION

My Guardians continued to explain: "The most expedient way for you to maximize effectiveness is to reverently and vibrationally align with your Higher Self daily. This means actively meditating and clearing your mind, so your Higher Self can "recharge" you. You recharge your devices nightly ... this is the same idea.

And yes, it does require that you tend to your human regimens ...that you eat well and get enough sleep and exercise. These activities optimize your ability to attain the frequency of vibration that invites clear communication. But in saying that to you we do recognize that the challenge for you in human form is to sustain those protocols. However, the more you do so, the clearer this communication with your loved ones can be, and the more effective your ability to attract will be – they go hand-in-hand. But we do not hold you to that higher standard. We can just assure you that there ARE specific, exponential results when you do."

I know that sounds easy, but as most of us know, it isn't. There were, and are, many starts and restarts to this ongoing commitment. I understand that this is part of being human, but I can also tell you the more I show up for my earthly commitments, the more momentum I have to sustain the receptive vibration. This concept is consistently referenced in *The Teachings of Abraham*. The more committed and consistent I was, the clearer my connection was, both to John and my Guidance. But again, I wasn't (and am not) perfect. As I progressed, I realized more and more how essential self-acceptance and love were. Shame, judgment, fear ... any "lower" vibrational feeling that I didn't resolve simply slowed this whole process down.

PAST LIFE REFERENCE

One day when John and I were out for our "walk and talk" he brought up a rather sensitive subject, but where he went with the topic was very surprising. I didn't expect that kind of wisdom.

Okay, Cath, this was interesting ... last night in your class, I was watching you. You were in your element. You're a teacher ... a facilitator. You have a lot of things to say ... a lot of wisdom. But there is some subtle way you don't fully step into that energy. It's as if you're a little "too" humble, he chuckles sarcastically.

Again, that comment surprised me. For one, it confirmed this feeling that he was right there watching me as I had felt so many times. Often I would remark to my husband that sometimes I felt we were this "reality show" for the other side!

But I was also very curious, then, about this feeling I sometimes have that I'm not fully seen by others. I wondered if he had any feedback about whether that feeling had anything to do with how often I felt unseen in our family. His response was interesting in that he referenced a component I would not have expected.

Well, it does have to do with that, somewhat, but there's a deeper wound for you that you have not adequately addressed ... a fragment that goes back to a Soul loss you have from a lifetime with the Spirit Guide you refer to as "Chief." That experience has not been resolved, and until it is you cannot be seen fully by others. I'm told this is one of the pieces of work you and I will do together – to retrieve her (that Soul fragment) and to work with her. I can help you with that. I can direct you to the right spot. We're being groomed for bigger conversations like that.

This conversation held a special interest for me especially when he began to reference that past life that involved "Chief." I have written an entire book about Chief, *Which Lifetime Is This Anyway?* A story I lived in 1992, and wrote in 2006, it depicts a shamanic tale of my continued relationship with my father after his death. It was during that experience that I first met Chief. He appeared right after Dad died to tell me Dad was going to be alright.

I initially thought Chief was Dad's Guardian Angel, but it was later revealed that Chief was, in fact, Dad's Higher Self. The lifetime John was referencing was another one that Chief and I shared when I was a Medicine Woman. Because of false accusations, I was banished from the tribe and left to perish. I had touched on this lifetime before but had never fully "resolved" it. As I began to work with the residue, I began to see how that banishment held the energetic blueprint of the banishment I experienced in this lifetime. John was trying to get me to connect the dots between that lifetime and this one.

Multidimensional healing often happens in layers. So, it didn't surprise me to be told there was another layer surfacing. My work with that layer is not relevant to this story, but it was relevant to my expansion. However, what is worthwhile to address is the fact that I continued to communicate with both Dad and Mom after their deaths. Each of those experiences depicts a different agenda or purpose for continued contact with a loved one once they're gone.

With Dad, it was very purposeful. The lifetime illustrated

in my book was one that Dad, in his afterlife, contacted me to address. I was meditating and Dad came into my mind's eye and very distinctly explained that HE needed to "heal" our issues from that lifetime before HE could progress as a Soul. This occurred in 1992, four years after Dad died. The fact that he *approached me* affirmed, at least to me, that Souls do continue to grow after death. And even though I was not as advanced then as I am today in these matters, I was, nonetheless, curious enough to pursue the contact, which again, is chronicled in *Which Lifetime Is This Anyway?*

However, what is relevant here is that, from what I gathered, continued communication with a loved one occurs for a variety of reasons. John and I have a specific, pre-determined agenda. Yet, on the other hand, my continued contact with Mom was different than my continued contact with John or Dad. With Mom it was more typical of what continued contact with a loved one usually is … she would jump into my consciousness to check up on me. Only once did she come to me with a request.

It happened one night in a dream. She came to tell me that I needed to relay to her best friend, Betty, that when it was time for Betty to make her transition from life to death, that Mom would be there as her guide. Mom was very insistent on my communicating that to Betty. It impressed me that when I did see Betty the next time and told her about this dream, she replied, "Yes, that does not surprise me!"

SO, JOHN, WHAT HAVE YOU LEARNED ABOUT KARMA?

John and I were beginning to get into some deeper conversations that were not specifically related to us. Sometimes he would take us there, but other times I would initiate a subject. This led us one day into the subject of "karma."

Now that's a whole new topic, he said, with a smile. *I'm being taught that some Souls that reincarnate are operating under an expanded color even though there's karma left. As we're doing our life-planning we have a choice to bring certain karmic themes through in the lifetime being planned. Many times, we do not. Often there's a series of lifetimes during which the Soul is gaining enough strength to take on its more serious Soul lessons.*

For instance, Cath, you KNEW you chose to deal with a lot of what happened to you ... you even told me that when I was alive ... you shared that story with me once about how you were told your Soul agreed to a series of events you would experience in this lifetime so you could clean up a lot of old issues. You knew that early in your adult life. That's why you were able, so early, to see the difference between "being a student of our experiences instead of a victim" to them. I notice you use that phrase often.

But this brings up something important, and that is that not everybody incarnates to learn the same lessons. Think of it in terms of the school structure. Some people that appear shallow incarnated to take what would appear to be "extra-curricular classes" ... and are not meant to spiritually expand a great deal in this physical form. That, I guess, is divinely decided. I'm also told that this can be determined, altered, or renegotiated as life progresses. But, as you've heard, no Soul NEEDS to be a victim to their circumstances. Each person is given the opportunity to elevate above hardship and expand because of it.

VISIT TO NEBRASKA

Shortly thereafter I traveled back to Nebraska to attend my older brother's annual Rib Fest and Concert. I was able to reconnect with friends I had not seen since John's memorial and see my brother, Tom, and my nieces and their children. But it was a special pleasure to sit and have a beer with one of John's dear friends who had been unable to attend John's *Celebration of Life.*

Larry graduated with John. His life had taken him to different parts of the world, but he always sustained contact with John. Every year on his sojourn back to the states Larry contacted John. He also contacted me. He had lived in San Francisco for a few years when I still lived there, and we had established a "like-minded" friendship. Larry was one with whom I could speak freely about this budding non-physical relationship with John. It was refreshing to share the experience with someone who not only knew John but showed a genuine interest in hearing about my continued relationship with him.

As Larry listened to me talk about the interactions I'd had with John since his passing, he very sincerely asked, "So if I wanted to have contact with John how would I do that?" The earnestness of his question touched me deeply and paved the way for continued conversations even when he had returned to his home in Thailand.

But this was not the only meaningful exchange of that trip. John's presence seemed even more profound during this event. For instance, I joined Tom and his band as they rehearsed for their upcoming performance. At one point when Tom started singing, I felt John standing behind me with his hands on my shoulders. It was so intense it sent chills down my back. Then, precisely at that moment, my eyes diverted to this large sign that said, "Taylor's." It startled me: It was the neon sign that Tom had on the outside of the restaurant he owned for over eighteen years.

For some reason, Tom had hung the sign in this bar after he had closed his restaurant several years earlier. I hadn't noticed it until then, but suddenly it was this flashing confirmation that John was there. Later Tom told me he felt John's presence as well. As was the case for John and me, there was a history between Tom and John. This gesture was a true sign that they had, indeed, elevated beyond their conflict.

But I felt John the next night, as well. It was at the concert. Tom's band was playing, and he's the lead vocalist. I was sitting on the bench with my niece's boys. Suddenly, I felt him behind me again, but this time I sensed this overwhelming gesture of brotherly pride. When I was driving back to Minnesota the next day, I took advantage of the long hours on the road to ask John about these experiences. I found his response, to say the least, illuminating.

> *Well, first ... I WAS standing behind you, and I usually don't get that close to you, but ... well ... it's hard to explain because I'm no longer limited by physical form ... but usually, my energy field is approaching you from the front ... which you would experience as heart to heart. But in those two experiences, you're right, I WAS energetically standing right behind you. You "perceived" that experience as my having my hands on your shoulders, which was appropriate. That was my intention. I wanted to give you that blanketed feeling. The chill you felt was your receptivity to me in that fashion. It was like an energetic confirmation from you to me that you had literally "received" my gesture.*

I teared up. I started to speak, but my voice cracked. The words I wanted to say never got out of my mouth before John continued.

> *That brotherly pride you felt in response to Tom and me,*

I Think... I Like You Better... Dead

and the emotion you feel now about it, is just an extension of your role as our sister. You're MY portal ... but in that experience, you provided a stronger bridge between Tom and me. In other words, Tom's experience was more profound because I could be more tangible due to our established connection.

Mom was there too. She wanted to experience that energetic reunion. But as you have gathered, both Mom and Dad have moved into their respective endeavors. We don't have much need to connect, but there ARE moments that we come together... moments that vibrationally call us into communion with one another. For instance, Mom always shows up for births. But what I really want you to get is that in situations such as this, the connection to others is always stronger when you're there because you call on us more ... you're a portal for all of us to gather. You're a link because of your receptivity. You're willing to feel us ... to believe in us and our presence. You can expand and meet us where our energy fields can mesh and you can sense each of us, separately, and as a family unit.

A Shift ... From What Was to What Would Be

I returned from Nebraska feeling a deeper sense of connection. But over the next several months I could feel a shift. It was subtle. At first it was just a little harder to "find" John. I couldn't quite reach him as I had been connecting with him. And of course, I assumed it was me. I felt uneasy and wondered if it was because I was so preoccupied with other things going on in my life. I had this nagging feeling I was doing something wrong. But then one day, John came through crystal clear and gave me the clue.

*Okay, I know you're unsettled, but here's what's happening.
We ARE going through an adjustment. You WILL feel as
though you don't know how to align with me. But,* he kind
of chuckles, *it has to do with me, not you. I'm going through
kind of a serious evolution now where I'm trying on my "Angel
wings"...* He flashed that shit-eating grin, once again. *We're
experimenting ... so just hang on. There's something big
coming ... so just hang on.*

And then he was gone. He was doing this more often now
... coming in and out rather abruptly. I would be engaged in
our connection and then suddenly, poof – his energy was gone.
I suspected, however, since there is no time on the other side, he
didn't relate this as disruptive. The only trouble for me with his
timing was that sometimes it would catch me off guard. I would
be engaged in something else, and suddenly his presence would
be so compelling that I would have to radically switch gears. It
wasn't intrusive *per se* ... but his timing was certainly according
to his schedule, not mine. Although, that had always been part
of John's demeanor. I would have thought, however, that it might
have evened out a bit as he became more "enlightened." Yet, truth
be told, it kept a slice of his old personality intact, so I always
knew it was him and not some other spirit trying to infringe. The
next time he "dropped in" he was exceptionally enthusiastic.

CLASS ON MULTIDIMENSIONALITY

I have some really cool things to tell you. In fact, he said
quite authoritatively, *you might want to take notes. You
have often asked me what I do up here ... so you're going to
find this interesting. I have been attending this multidimensional class ... learning about the levels of consciousness and
reviewing what you and I are being instructed to do. And*

God, Cath, I realize there is so much more to who I am ... and who I am to you ... than I ever imagined. Once we get our book finished, I'll be able to share so much more with you ... direct information that's not relevant to this book. But let's talk for a minute about the book because this part does relate.

People on Earth just don't realize how thin the veil is if the human is willing to believe it ... to really believe it. If a person can believe the other side is so close, they can take advantage of that closeness, and their life can be so enriched. So many of us want to work hand in hand with our loved ones, but the barrier of disbelief is so hard to penetrate.

What does influence this though is the practice of meditation. That really is the vehicle through which the barrier can be penetrated. You've experienced that. The more you meditate and strengthen that muscle of expansion, the clearer our connection is. But even you struggle with this. You make it either / or ... like I have elevated now to this new, higher dimension, so I'm no longer recognizable as your brother. But let me explain something to you ... you're going to love this ... it's all a continuum.

THE CONTINUUM

Here's what I just learned. I CAN TRAVEL a continuum just like you guide your clients to travel that continuum from their adult self to their inner child and then back up to their Higher Self. That's why your method of inner child and Soul work is effective ... you guide your clients to move up and down the continuity of their vibrational existence by separating from the different dimensional representations that exist. Then you teach them how to INTERACT with the different dimensional parts of who they are ... body and Soul. That's the beauty of your work.

So that's exactly what I have been shown I can do on a Soul level. I told you awhile back I was being guided through my "Soul review." It's common to think of the "life review," but remember, I mentioned how I was being "escorted" through every expression my Soul had ever been. My Teachers wanted me to begin to see the themes, patterns, and lessons, I have encountered and still need to master.

Ok, so that's all very cool. But what that means in terms of our relationship is that at any given moment, I can relate to you from any place I have ever been. I can connect with you from that brother John vibration, or I can connect with you from the vibration of who I was in another body or time. But I can also relate to you from my purest form of frequency when you're aligned enough to connect with me there. You're not always there ... some days you spin out or you're distracted and don't even recognize it is me connecting with you because you're not able to "read" my energy. But this is part of what you and I will be getting "trained" to do ... is to come into alignment with higher and higher vibrational frequencies.

Okay, think of it this way: for most of our post-life experiences we have been focusing on how you and I can reach the resonance that enables you to feel me, and me to feel you. We have been learning how to bridge the gap of the veil and meet there.

But what they're going to start working with us on next is you actually letting go of your ego enough so I can BRING you more and more to THIS side of the veil. So, yes, you're my portal on your side of the veil, but I'm your periscope to this side. Now there is some reconfiguration that has to take place, and I haven't been shown how that is going to happen yet.

He was talking so fast ... I was beginning to feel a bit overwhelmed. I was trying to catch all of this – I mean, I understood what he was saying in theory, but was he talking about astral projection here, or what?

"Okay, okay, John, slow down ... I need a minute here. I think I'm getting this, but *Jesus*, can you just take a coffee break or something and give me a moment to digest this?"

We both laughed.

Yeah, yeah ... of course ... just breathe for a moment ... you're right ... you're starting to fog out on me. But really, Cath, stay with me here. You, more than anyone, should get this because this is what you're doing all the time in your work. We're just linking it for you now Soul to Soul.

He was right. This was a lot to take in, but it tickled me that he was again so directive. However, I never could have predicted where he was going to take us next. I'd never seen John so fired up about anything before. He continued speaking about what he had learned and where we were going to go.

YOU MAY BE MY PORTAL ... BUT I'M YOUR PERISCOPE

Now, when I said I wasn't ever going to leave you I meant that. You will never have to be without me as your brother ... as you knew me when I was alive. Just like you have felt so far, when you do something stupid, those typical Cathy antics of yours, you will still hear me make some crack just as if I were standing right next to you in your time and space. That's what keeps me real. That enables me to experience things through you as my portal.

B U T ... here's the cool part ... just as you're my portal ... I'm YOUR PERISCOPE.

As we "grow" together I will be able to take you to so many other versions that we have been ... and maybe even will be. I don't know, this is all still a little new to me, but, I'm told that when you trust me enough to let go of your ego a little more, you will let me guide you to non-physical places ... where you'll feel formless, bodiless.

That's why your meditations are so important. It's during those times I can help you expand to a higher level of vibrational consciousness where we relate as Soul energies SO MUCH BEYOND John and Cathy. There's just so much more! AND, ultimately, I will be able to take you on all kinds of journeys, because as your Ambassador, I'm told I will be trained to also be your travel guide into other dimensions. But you're going to have to let go of that ego a little bit more before we can do that. You still want to retain control, but as you trust me, you will soften with that... all in good time, I'm told! And there may be a point of transition where you feel like you've lost me ... and honestly, that will not be the case.

But you wouldn't believe how many on this side relate to what you and I are doing. We're not really talking about anything new, such as concepts or anything ... but what we ARE going to demonstrate to others is how they can create partnerships with their loved ones after they're dead. As this project progresses, you'll see how we're being "schooled" to be an example of what it can be like when the human is willing to operate as a portal and be receptive to their loved one being their periscope. That's why this book is relevant. It will open doors for others to use their relationships with their loved ones to bridge the veil and experience the multiple dimensions of their relationships to their loved ones even after they have died.

But There IS Going to Be a Transition

You have already started to feel a shift, and you might find it a little difficult. But in order to get to where we need to go you ARE going to have to let go of me as John for a while ... not for long ... but for a short time so those new dimensional pathways can be forged. That's coming up soon, so don't be alarmed. Don't be afraid. I'll still be with you. It will just take some adjustment to vibrationally recalibrate as we go through this transition.

But I guarantee you will have plenty of support when this happens. In fact, wait until you see how this is going to take place. It'll blow your mind. We'll slowly begin to focus on the end of the continuum of formlessness. BUT ... you're going to love this ... once we establish that new alignment, we will be free to slide up and down the continuum.

So, what does that mean?

I'll have the capacity to relate to you from that all-personality-on-board self you knew me to be as your brother. We'll be able to recognize each other at the earth-plane frequencies as well as the Soul frequencies. We won't be bound by one vibrational signature of each other.

Expanded Vibrational Signatures

What was taught in this class is that every vibrational expression of us continues to exist. That's why when you take others back in time to an inner child or another part of their

Soul you can always help them access the vibration of the person they were. Those regressions are more than just memories, or one's imagination. The client is actually returning to "relate" to another vibrational expression of who they were at that time. Those vibrational impressions exist on that continuum. It's not only true for the "fractured" parts of the Soul, or even aspects of the personality from the current lifetime that can be retrieved and healed. It's true for every dimensional expression we've ever been. They all continue to exist.

So, there will always be an expression of me as your brother, John, that you can access. BUT ... and this is a big "but" ... as we begin to explore the Universe together, we will get to know the other expressions of who we have been all along the trajectory of our Soul's journey. It's endless, Cath, and so multifaceted it will blow your mind.

But we ARE coming up on a time when again, you'll FEEL you can't access me ... like you have lost me. But I'm here to tell you that nothing will be further from the truth. We're just going to be getting a vibrational upgrade. You'll see ... you'll see what I mean when that time comes.

And then, once again he was gone. But this conversation, to say the least, left me dumbfounded, exhilarated, and a bit apprehensive. He *was* right: The vibrational resonance *did* begin to change, and even though *I knew what I knew*, and John *had predicted* the vibrational shift, when it happened, I did feel a void. There was a sense of loss and sadness that our connection had diminished. But that didn't last long. As John promised, I soon saw what he meant about the vibrational upgrade. And once that occurred, there was an expansion available to us that was beyond measure!

PART FOUR:
"HEALINGS BEYOND THE VEIL"

Cathryn Taylor's writing creates echoes in our souls of what is true and leads us deeply into the process of transformation. Keep "I Think I Like You Better Dead" close by, and dip in whenever you want to nourish your spirit.

Christina Chironna, Film Producer | Founder & COO at FilmUp
www.filmup.co

YOUR THOUGHTS AND COMMENTS:

_____

_____

_____

_____

_____

_____

_____

_____

_____

_____

_____

_____

_____

_____

_____

_____

_____

_____

CHAPTER ELEVEN:
DOWN THE RABBIT HOLE /
THROUGH THE TUNNEL

MY FAVORITE INTERVIEW OF THE FALL

I ALWAYS LOOK FORWARD to the fall lineup of interviews I conduct on behalf of the Edge Talk Radio (for which I am a staff member), because every October I get to interview Christine Day. Known as the Ambassador of the Pleiadians, a group of advanced alien beings intending to assist humans and the planet earth in our ascension and evolution, Christine shares their messages that offer support and energetic practices to assist us as we experience frequency upgrades. Christine is devoted to assisting us in understanding and responding to the energetic changes taking place within us, and on the planet, at this time in the evolution of our consciousness.

The fall of 2019 was no exception. Christine was preparing to present her annual gathering of multidimensional, energetic initiations from the Pleiadians. That year's program was to assist participants in gaining a deeper remembrance of their sacred Higher Self. One of the perks of our interview was that Christine always extended an invitation to me to attend, which I gladly and gratefully accepted.

The event was scheduled for November 2-4, two days before the first-year anniversary of John's passing. We had experienced many exchanges in that first year, but John had warned me that an upgrade was on the way. I suspected Christine's seminar would be the place in which that would take place. I was not wrong. Christine and I had spoken about the situation with John several times, so when she greeted me at the registration table, she was not surprised to hear I was coming upon the year's anniversary of his passing. Without hesitation, she said, "Your brother is here. Keep the chair next to you empty so you can sense his energy because the two of you are to realign your vibrational resonance."

The seminar was profound. We were guided through initiations to realign us with our crystalline body frequency.

As the flyer predicted:

"This frequency, referred to as the "Merkaba," is made up of a pure crystalline liquid light, and as it births or realigns, it naturally anchors through different areas of the body — from the sacrum, the spinal fluid, the brain stem, the pineal, and the heart. At the same time, this process is designed to work within the brain-spine axis and central nervous system to enhance the brain's functioning. As the Merkaba body is anchored it activates the brain-spine axis and reopens areas of the brain that have not been activated in this lifetime. It is like an electrical redesign of the system, and all the cells in the physical body will be switched on from a very different multidimensional perspective."

Needless to say, the experience promised to be, and was, quite powerful and prepared me on a cellular level to have the following upgrading experience.

FROM THE RABBIT HOLE TO THE TUNNEL

After sufficient realignments and initiations, we were invited to enter into this sacred circle of crystals. A series of chairs geometrically placed further created the sacred portal for transformation. Once each of us had found our divine place in this configuration Christine began to chant. We were then invited to go into our own meditation.

I had no idea what to expect, but the minute I sat down I began to feel a surge of energy ripple through my body. Then I began to hear John's voice calling me. At first, I could only see that I was entering the far end of a tunnel ... a tunnel like what we hear described by those who report near death experiences.

I felt apprehensive, but at the far end of the tunnel, I could see light ... and an opening ... and I began to hear John's voice calling to me ... encouraging me to proceed ... assuring me it was safe.

I slowly followed the sound of his voice as I moved through the tunnel. His face emerged. It was comforting. And the movement ... it was effortless, as if I was on a conveyor belt being pulled along. I felt a moment of trepidation and the movement gently slowed down. "Okay, good," I say to myself. "I seem to be in control of the pace."

Then, again I heard John's voice, calmly assuring me.

Come on Cath, it's safe. I'm here. Just let go.

And then, instantaneously, I was through the tunnel and was standing on what felt like this bed of light. Slowly, John's image emerged. He gave what felt like this great big bear hug. I felt lighter. I still had a sense of form, but I was definitely lighter.

And the hug, it felt more like a merger of energy than my form touching his form. It was an odd sensation, and one I'd never experienced in the density of my body. John was smiling and full of excitement that I'd finally let go enough to arrive.

"John," I ask, "am I on the other side?" I could hear my words, but my mouth didn't move ... it was telepathic, formulated thought to thought.

It's okay, you're fine, he replied.

Then, quite by surprise, I began to see all these other beings appear ... beings I had known from this side. They were greeting me ... welcoming me. I momentarily felt this fear that perhaps I died, but just as soon as that thought emerged, John assured me that was not the case.

No, you're okay ... but you will never again be the same. This is the last time you will be 'dependent' upon my vibration as your brother to communicate with me. It's not that you won't sense me in that brotherly vibration, but this signature is a whole new frequency for us. It is the vibration we needed to attain for us to be able to go on the journeys we are to now explore. And there are other vibrational shifts to be made. This is just a beginning.

Then just as quickly as I had moved through the tunnel, I was back sitting in my chair and the experience was over. I could hear Christine's voice calling us to leave the sacred circle and return to our chairs.

Additional processes occurred after this experience, but my focus remained on integrating what had just happened. It's not that I did not take in additional pointers and initiations, but my conscious focus remained on this exchange, integrating what had taken place, adjusting and anchoring. At one of the breaks I conferred with Christine. She validated that my experience was real and that, in fact, this was the very purpose John and I were guided to attend this seminar. Our mission had been completed.

JOHN'S FIRST ANNIVERSARY

Two days later, on John's first year anniversary I was still energetically integrating the experience at Christine's seminar. I went into my meditation, aligned my cellular structure to match our multidimensional structure, and dissolved the veil between us. I could feel the anchoring of all past life memory—of all future memory and of all present tasks.

Today, on the anniversary of your releasing your physical form, we are celebrating (tears are rolling down my cheeks) the integration and our partnership.

And the opening of my heart, the opening of my throat chakra, my third eye, my crown, my solar plexus, my root chakra to better receive you, hear you, be inspired by you to write our book.

There's so much more that I now understand ... the purpose of my holding the vibrational momentum for you as you stepped in and out of the new dimension according to your own karma. And how you used me as a touchstone at those beneficial moments. I understand now why you had to turn away from me to complete your karma with Keri so she would have the opportunity to step up without being in the middle of our dialogue. I understand your rejections from a new vantage point.

And now we are coming into a commitment our Souls made before we even took our physical forms this time around. This last year has been testament to that commitment. And each day I can show up for this continued relationship, the essence of commitment becomes clearer. Is there any block I need to address to move forward? I took a deep breath, and then sensed John's response.

It's okay, Cath. There's no pressure in terms of your writing our book. It will flow when it flows. You've seen that with your other pieces of work. Your biggest block is just trust. Just give up the idea that you need to struggle. That's the biggest piece I can say is just give up the struggle. Give up the negativity ... any doubt. It is what it is.

That's what really being on the other side of the veil is all about. You give it all up. When we let go of our physical form, we get to give up the negativity. And the more you align with your etheric or crystalline body, and the more that we hang out, the more accepting you're going to be — and the more trusting — the more knowing. You asked for the block. What's the block? It's just, give up the struggle, enjoy. Interesting, huh?

I loved every page and every page kept me engaged and turning to the next. This book is phenomenal in its timeliness for guidance and references to how to gracefully move where we co-create our lives with energy and guidance from all levels.

Jennifer Forest, Co-Owner www.siennaosv.com

YOUR THOUGHTS AND COMMENTS:

_____

_____

_____

_____

_____

_____

_____

_____

_____

_____

_____

_____

_____

_____

_____

_____

_____

_____

_____

CHAPTER TWELVE:
ALICIA'S SPIRIT SURGEONS, TEACHERS, AND CREATOR BEINGS

ELEVATOR ESCAPADES

THE CHAIN OF events that followed suggested that our relationship was being primed for an upgrade as John's role, progressively and almost unnoticeably, shapeshifted from Ambassador to co-partner and collaborator. It happened as we were "guided" through a series of "conjoint trainings" that gave birth to a relationship based on reciprocity and equality. I began to appreciate the fact that John had his role, and I equally had mine.

This shift came one afternoon when I was sitting at my computer working on a report. Suddenly I felt an uncontrollable urgency to check my inbox. I scrolled through my emails and was drawn to one from Ian Shelley promoting his current Summit entitled, *Wisdom of the Ancients*. I had no idea how his email had reached me because, up until that very moment, I had never heard of Ian or his Summit. But there *it* was … and there

I was ... experiencing this overwhelming nudge to purchase his entire package.

The next step came just as effortlessly. As I skimmed through the presenters my eye was drawn to a presentation recently conducted by Alicia Power. Again, I had never heard of Alicia, but this description of her presentation, quoted directly from Ian's email, appealed to me.

> *Alicia Power has spent over 30 years dialoging clearly with spirit tutors who bring a deep understanding of how life works. Enjoy learning from a Master Healer and soul 'archaeologist'. Hear Alicia's recent full 1-hour lecture to an international audience.*

I dropped what I was doing and listened intently to her interview. Immediately I felt uplifted, not only by her discussion, but also by her 13-minute sample healing. There was no resistance to allowing Alicia's spiritual surgeons to work on my force field. It was one of those "you had me at hello" experiences. Her "Special Offer" was equally attractive.

> *These advanced and accelerated Spirit Technician 're-wiring' sessions, called Creator Light Surgery, are real. They'll take you deep straight away.*
>
> *The more you switch on your attention during the session the FASTER & DEEPER your SHIFT will be. If you allow yourself to enjoy a 10 min meditation beforehand, your experience WILL be exponentially more powerful. BE READY TO DANCE IN THE LIGHT OF POWERFUL HEALING....*

It made total sense to me this was the next stage of John's and my training, but, at that time, I had no clue as to how deep these clearings and adjustments would actually be. Yet, there was no doubt that I was directed to Alicia's work via an inter-dimensional, telepathic vibration that was now available to John and me. Even Alicia's domain name (www.soulmentoring.com) was compelling. I grabbed my credit card and "enrolled us" in a series of courses.

In our next *official* meditation John was gleaming as he confirmed, *Yes, Cath, this is exactly the level of schooling we need to build on what we experienced in Christine's seminar. I'm telling you ... these technicians are the real deal! They are going to reconfigure our electromagnetic fields so we can be more telepathically aligned and develop more effective ways to work, teach, and explore together. I am told our trainings will prepare us to walk in tandem with the pre-destined roles our Souls agreed to a long time ago. This is big, Cath, bigger than either of us had imagined.*

John went on to emphatically explain that this was evidence of how in sync we had now become.

Okay, listen to this, Cath ... because it is so important, and I want to make sure you really understand this. I wouldn't have been successful at this gesture if you hadn't expanded the frequency of vibrational resonance that we now have mutually created. I've gotten better at sending you an impulse, but your receptivity has grown as well. It's an example of how you are bridging from your third dimension of reality to that fifth dimension. This is exactly what we, in the non-physical, have to offer our loved ones who are still in the physical dimension.

This is that reciprocity you've been feeling ever since you trusted me enough to move beyond your ego and experience me on this side of the veil. It is a collaborative experience. You and I can't get to where we're destined to go now without a shared investment and the "vibrational capacity" to read each other. And that requires your "continued" willingness to expand beyond your fear and doubt of that third dimension, using the love you feel for me in the fifth.

Okay, so this is what I have been told ... it's going to get even more intense. Through these healings and surgeries the obstacles within us and between us will be cleared and repro-grammed so we, together, can construct our unique bridge between the two dimensions ... a "sustainable" dissolution of the veil ... and the separation between the physical and the non-physical. We had a taste of it in the meditation we experienced in Christine's class, but just wait and see ... these trainings are going to clear our paths so we can enhance our mutual ability beyond what either of us could ever predict!

And it's going to provide an example, Cath, of what relationships such as these can achieve. There are so many up here that have contracts similar to ours. Their loved ones in your dimension just need the inspiration and direction on how to pursue them. That's just a glimpse of the bigger picture of what our book will illustrate ... a story that offers those who are earthbound just that ... pretty cool, huh?

John continued, with such a sense of excitement, to give me a detailed report of how he was guided to this next step. The manner in which his Guardians were *contacted* by those who work with Alicia, then *guided to connect* with her energy in the unseen, and subsequently *instructed* to work hand-in-hand with *my* Guardians to *inspire* me to find her work on this plane felt like a scene directed by Steven Spielberg or Ron Howard. It was absolutely astounding. And to be honest, this entire conversation left me speechless. But it soon became clear John and I were being invited into a partnership that would span the two dimensions of time and that Alicia's spiritual technicians were going to work with us to make that happen. In a later check-in session with

Samantha, John again relayed how excited he was about this development.

> *"John wants you to know how amazed he was at how quickly you followed his promptings ... and how much better the two of you are at communicating telepathically."* He says,
>
> with such passion, *"It's instantaneous ... little time delay at all! And it's only going to get better!"*

Although not as greatly needed as in the early days of our continued relationship, Samantha's confirmation was once again comforting. The fact that John and I had finally reached the point in our relationship when we would be schooled to *work together* as a team ... irrespective of the gap in our dimensional realities ... was exhilarating. It was feeling more and more surreal, like something I had only seen in movies like *What Dreams May Come*.

I mean ... I knew it was coming. I had experienced glimpses that we were moving toward this level of partnership but to actually *experience* that degree of communication left me feeling giddy ... almost childlike ... with excitement and anticipation. Yet, what was even more curious was that the training itself was so gradual, and gradient, that the reality of this advancement became less and less unusual, and more and more real.

NINETY DAYS OF "BOOT CAMP"

The next three months were spent submerging ourselves in a variety of healings and clearings. Each day followed the same structure. I would align to my Soul and then step into the proverbial, vibrational elevator where John was always waiting.

The minute the elevator began to move we would hear the voice of Alicia directing us to the appropriate floor of consciousness. Her voice spoke to my Soul in the same soothing and assuring way clients tell me my voice speaks to their inner child. It always provided the exact vibration that would connect John and I to the level of consciousness where her Spirit Teachers, Surgeons, and high-level Creator Beings could greet us and begin the work scheduled for that day.

Initially they worked on us separately, but simultaneously. We would respectively be put into the appropriate healing chamber where our personal Soul patterns could be rewired and released. Our respective, energetic systems were recalibrated to ultimately effectuate our work together and apart.

I recalled this level of healing taking place early in my metaphysical studies. I would be met by spiritual teachers and taken through a series of light-infused healings preparing my psyche ... body, mind, heart, and Soul ... for my life's work. But this level of healing was being conducted by a much higher and more specific authority of technicians. Whereas my early-day healings that occurred in the early 1980s, had prepared me to teach in this world and cleared the energetic field that encased my Soul as Cathryn Taylor, *these healings* were burrowing deep into the crevasses of the Akashic Record of my Soul, beyond what was relevant to just this lifetime.

This high level of healing was simultaneously clearing John and I so we would ultimately be equipped to cross the inter-dimensional barrier that would allow us to fulfill the contract of our Souls. And even though Alicia's voice initially provided the bridge needed to connect us across the veil, the trainings we experienced in those three months enabled John and I to build our own bridge that strengthened our capacity to create the platform needed to sustain the connection on our own.

But again ... the progression was gradual ... and ever-so gentle.

OUR SOUL RELATIONSHIP GETS AN UPGRADE

Once our personal Soul patterns had been sufficiently cleared and rewired the healings shifted to address our combined energies. It became evident that this book was not going to be "downloaded" to me from John or his teachers ... any more than it was going to be "channeled" to me through *my* Akashic Records.

The spirit surgeons and technicians began fortifying us as partners ... as a team. John's role progressively shifted from that of Ambassador to that of partner. Our forcefields were rewired, adjusted, reconfigured as the healings and surgeries forged a blended vibrational signature which prepared us to co-create collaboratively. Our relationship began operating as this unit that could *surf the continuum* of all we had ever been. *And,* what was, and continues to be, absolutely "delicious" about this evolution is that by the time we got to the writing of this last part of the book, there was, in fact, *no separation* to bridge.

I have no attachment to how John and I connect. We have the freedom to relate with the familiarity we experienced as brother and sister because that essence of who we are to each other in this very dimension has been secured. We have attained the telepathic and etheric frequency which enables us to work in tandem ...

pulsating ideas and exchanges without need for translation. The transmissions between us are immediate. There truly is no separation. I can't emphasize that enough. We have complete access to each other through the pure impulse of thought.

It's amazing, uplifting, and I believe a concrete illustration of what it feels like to have the portal between the third and fifth dimensions fluidly open. Furthermore, I am beginning to understand what John had suggested ... that this is the true gift and contribution our deceased loved ones can offer us, individually, and to humanity, collectively.

Once we *believe* in their existence; lose our *need* for, and *attachment to*, them staying connected to us as they were when they were here; courageously navigate through the grief and adjustments needed to extend beyond our own ego; we *can* develop the "capacity" to meet our loved ones at any point on the continuum of where we have ever been ... in any time and space. We develop our ability to step into the true multiple dimensions ... to meet our loved ones ... with no attachment ... at any juncture ... on the continuum that stretches from the physical to the nonphysical dimensions with ease and complete confidence.

Having known Cathryn for over three decades I can truly say she writes from the heart. But ... the information she and John bring to us through their story is fresh ... authentic ... and absolutely astounding.

Laurel King,
Co-author with Shakti Gawain of *Living in the Light*
And author of *Women of Power*
and *Whistling Woman Up To No Good*

Your Thoughts and Comments:

_____

_____

_____

_____

_____

_____

_____

_____

_____

_____

_____

_____

_____

_____

_____

_____

_____

_____

_____

CHAPTER THIRTEEN:
WHAT THE WORLD
NEEDS NOW IS ...

THE BIGGER PICTURE

I BEGAN TO UNDERSTAND that the impact of this vibrational blend had the potential to reach far beyond the project itself. Yes, John and I had to find our way to the vibrational signature that enabled us to write this book, but it is this frequency at which our relationship is now sustained. This connection was the result of our commitment to do so and didn't happen overnight. Our ability to attain this level of connection was the result of hours of meditation and connection, confirmation from others, and a willingness on my part to believe and accept.

All dissonance that our healing with Alicia's spiritual tutors and surgeons had dislodged and removed was replaced with new consciousness software. We are able to telepathically, creatively, and spiritually partner with each other in any endeavor. Whenever I think of John, I feel he is there. If we collaborate with each other, we are merged. If we are hanging out together, there is no distance. He is always welcomed in my world, in my mind, with no sense of intrusion and yet, we have access to all the vibrational expressions we are and ever have been.

What lies ahead for us now is an exploration of those expressions, but also continued collaboration between the two worlds. Writing this book was just the first of many endeavors we have contracted to work on together. It is as if we are business partners in ways that benefit not only this world but as Abraham teaches, contributes to the creation in the non-physical one.

By the time we met in Christine's class I was able to allow John to "coax" me through the tunnel of my own ego ... just as he had let go of his ego at the time of his death. This high-level transformation not only changed John's and my capacity to blend our energy fields as a team, it also augmented my relationship to the non-physical world and to my Higher Self and Guardians in ways I can't even begin to describe. It is as if my sense of taste, sight, touch, smell, and sound was amplified in full living-color. My capacity to experience love, my heart-to-heart connection with my husband, family and friends, my ability to be present in my work, the manner in which I interact with nature, experience abundance in my life, and even the unrest in our world has been gravely broadened.

But perhaps the most heart-squeezing development for me is the incredible appreciation I have developed for the need to have this veil thinned at such a volatile time in the history of our planet. With that in mind, paramount to this experience and evident at this time, is my *knowingness* that the only way this can occur is if, individually and collectively, this higher level of consciousness can successfully lift us from the third dimension of fear to the fifth dimension of love. And, what has become so obvious to me is that as more and more of us are inspired and willing to let our loved ones escort us to a higher vibration that we can actively contribute, not only to our own transcendence, but to the evolution of our planet and humanity itself.

THE "TIMELY" ANNUAL INTERVIEW WITH CHRISTINE DAY

In the middle of completing the last section of this book it was again the time of the year when I had the privilege of speaking with Christine for our annual Edge Talk Radio interview. In response to the Coronavirus, the social and racial unrest, and the influx of fires, hurricanes, and other natural disasters, I couldn't help but ask for her unique perception of this upheaval. It was comforting to hear her speak about the intensity of light being transmitted to the planet at this time, which equals the need for the assistance as humanity and Mother Earth herself transition to a collective higher level of consciousness.

I have understood for a long time that whenever we, as individuals, expand and bring in a higher vibration of consciousness to our etheric and physical bodies that we also illuminate the shadow. We need to be prepared individually and collectively, to address this shadow and all that gets dislodged in response to it. She assured me that this was indeed what was happening to our planet and to our collective consciousness.

I was reminded of the weekend of August 16th – 17th, in 1987, when I attended the first global celebration called the "Harmonic Convergence." The dates coincided with an exceptional alignment of planets in the solar system. I recalled hearing at that time and, in fact, many times since then, about a prediction that I believe can at least be found in both the book of revelations and Hindu teachings forecasting that there would be an incarnation of 144,000 lightworkers who would escort the earth from the destruction of the world to the creation of a new cycle.

The most interesting part about that prediction was that

supposedly most of those lightworkers were already here and in the process of "waking up" to their divine purpose and mission on earth. I was one year shy of 40, but I knew from that day on I wanted to be one of them. I wanted to be one of those spiritual seekers to hold the vibration of light it would ultimately take to successfully make what is now referred to as the "dimensional shift from the third, and then through the fourth and fifth, dimensions of consciousness." I never forgot that event, or that invitation. I experienced it as a "call to service" and have been more seriously committed to my own spiritual awakening ever since.

Knowing that the kernel of Christine's work involves this process, I asked if she felt humanity had succeeded. I cannot tell you how relieved I was to hear her confirm that indeed, we have. Irrespective of how our planet gets to its next evolution, and regardless of how the shadow aspects of humanity and Mother Earth get dislodged, and ultimately resolved, it appears as though all of this is happening for a reason – and yes, she confirmed there is enough light now available to transmute and succeed.

I am still not clear whether the thinning of the veil between John and me was a *byproduct* of this progressive light infusion, a *contribution* to it, or a *combination* of both. However, this conversation certainly gave me a much deeper appreciation for our experience and an increased enthusiasm to share our story with the world.

JUST WHEN I THOUGHT WE WERE DONE

This understanding and recalibration inspired me to discuss this with John the next time we went on one of our "elevator excursions." This time we weren't taken "up" for a healing. Instead I found us once again walking and talking around the lake revisiting our shared experience of developing our book ... exploring together "where we'd been and where we'd ended up."

It reminded me of how my parents and grandparents would go on a trip and then return home with boxes and boxes of slides that documented their experience. The family would then be invited to a Sunday dinner, after which we were expected to enthusiastically watch the slideshow. I actually suggested to John that we take you, the reader, through such a slideshow of our experience. It didn't take him long to humorously remind me of how bored we had been at those infamous "Sunday dinners."

Jesus, Cath, I can't imagine how many cups of coffee it would take to keep anyone interested in that part of our story, no matter how interesting it is to you and me. Let's just save that activity for ... (he paused) ... for maybe the sequel.

"Save it for what?"

The sequel! He says with a laugh that starts from his belly and morphs into that shit-eating grin on his face.

"What sequel" I exclaim? "I'm not writing any damn sequel, John," I protest. "I am EXHAUSTED down here!"

But before I could go any further, we were again back in the elevator, ascending to the floor that would reveal what was to happen next.

Thank you, Cathryn, for sharing this work with me. I just read your Epilogue and I am moved to tears. My heart listens to your words and is so moved by your ability to call it into action in this invisible realm. It is close to separating from my chest by the vibration of SHEER JOY alone.
Melanie Kult, Friend and Confidant

EPILOGUE:
"TED TALK AT THE VEIL"

J OHN WAS RIGHT. What happened next was so obvious, yet so beyond what I'd ever had time to imagine. As the elevator came to a gentle stop and the doors opened, I could see we were at a lecture hall. The muted voices of people excitedly waiting for the program to commence began filtering into my awareness.

In an instant we're magically out of the elevator. I'm standing on one side of the stage ... John is waiting in the wings directly across from me. It dawns on me that John and I are the *featured* speakers, and even more curious is the fact that my friend and colleague, Brian Mariani, is on stage introducing us. It seems important to note that Brian exists in this third dimension. He's not dead. He's very much alive. And yet, there he is meeting John and I at the Veil.

I first was contacted by Brian several months after John's passing. Arthur and I were in Encinitas, California, for a winter vacation. My cell phone rang. Brian introduced himself by saying he'd gotten my number from my friend Timothy Cope who thought I might be interested in a business opportunity Brian was promoting. Still somewhat tender from the loss of John I briefly shared the situation explaining I was not in a position to consider such matters. I suggested we speak in a couple of months. "I'd love to talk on March 16th. That's my brother's birthday. John was always 'bugging' me to expand my business. It feels like hearing what you have to say on that day would be a nice way to honor him," I offered.

Two months later when Brian called, the first thing he asked was how I was doing? "I know this is a special day for you, and I want to acknowledge that before we talk about this opportunity." The fact that he remembered that ... and led with that ... impressed me. From then on, wherever Brian went, I followed.

This was true even two *years* later, when in response to the pandemic Brian and his family, who own the *Center for Functional Nutrition*, started a weekly Zoom meeting called the *Coffee House Virtual Gathering*. Not only was I invited to give a presentation on dealing with the varied feelings related to the Coronavirus, and at a later date to share my "Minneapolis" experience after George Floyd's death, it was also at the *Coffee House Gathering* that I made my first public presentation about John's and my adventure.

Of course, it made sense that Brian would be the emcee for this supposed "Introductory Lecture" ...

"I never knew Cathryn and John as brother and sister. But I've had the distinct pleasure of following Cathryn's journey *with* John for the last two years. Although it stretched my belief system, I knew, even if *I* didn't fully believe what I heard, that it was true for Cathryn. Through hearing her stories about her experiences with her brother, I feel like I know John almost as well as I now know her ...

So, you might not know *why* you're here ... but I can guarantee you will not be disappointed. Their adventures are not only entertaining ... for those of you who are open, they can be inspiring, transforming, and offer perhaps an invitation some part of you has long awaited.

So, without further ado, it is my pleasure to introduce you to Cathryn and John Taylor."

As we walk onto the stage, John catches my eye. He's got that infamous grin on his face as he telepathically shoots me the message ... *"Why did he give **you** top billing?"* I laugh, and reply ... "because I'm the one down here doing all the 'heavy lifting.' Remember, it's a lot easier for you to navigate through this stuff up there than me down here in this density." *Point well-taken!* He telepathically shoots back! "And by the way', I add, "it would've been nice to have had a dress rehearsal for this!" He throws me a soft nod with raised eyebrows.

It amuses me that no matter how far "up" this multi-dimensional road we travel together there is forever that sibling banter. It seems, in some way, to keep me grounded and able to function in this third-dimensional reality in which I live.

While this conversation is taking place telepathically, I simultaneously notice that even though *I'm* dressed in "Saks Fifth Avenue" attire, John has chosen to be a little more creative. As he walks towards me he first appears in his "Harvey" outfit ... which quickly morphs into his casual dress ... but by the time he meets me in the center of the stage he is appropriately dressed in professional garb. Yet, I have no time to inquire as to whether this fashion show is for my benefit only or something the entire audience can appreciate because my attention is immediately redirected to the patrons sitting in the seats before me.

As I look out over the sections of the lecture hall, I see there is further play on this "wardrobe display" that ripples through the entire audience. The closer to the stage the more opaque the dress of the attendee ... the further away the more translucent. There is an instant transmission from my Guardians explaining that those sitting in the orchestra section have paid the most for being there because the price of admission is based on the effort needed to overcome the resistance to attend.

"The more earthbound the attendee is to third dimensional beliefs," they explain, "the more it cost that person to attend. This is also why you're dressed in clothes that are vibrationally recognizable to those who resonate with your more fixed, human vibration. John's clothing could be more fluid and interchangeable. You see there needs to be an appropriate vibrational resonance for the patrons in both dimensions to identify with each of you respectively if they are to experience what is being offered at this joint meeting at the "Veil." In other words, think of both of you being used as tuning forks for your respective dimensions.

As I am listening to their explanation I glance up at the balcony. There is a constant stream of blinking lights representing the spirits that occupy that section. They have no physical bodies, no fees for seating … because they have absolutely no resistance to being there. I also notice there is no end to the balcony section. It continues as far, and actually further, than my eye can see.

My attention comes back to the words coming out of John's mouth. As he speaks each word is being transmitted in waves of energy that are modulated according to the frequency appropriate for each section. I've never experienced anything like this before. I mean, *I've* channeled words in other presentations, but I'd never witnessed the vibratory recalibration of words as they were being delivered to a multidimensional audience. Interesting, I thought, as my ears again tune into the words being spoken by John.

I was lucky, I had a sister who was way beyond me … so when I lifted up to the non-physical realm, she was willing to grab my hand. Those of you who sit in the sections closest to the stage … you are paying the highest price for your tickets,

*because you have the greatest distance to cover in your disbelief.
But what's important is that you chose to be here.*

*Cathryn is here to act as a bridge to your loved ones and
I'm here on behalf of those loved ones who sit in the tiers right
above you. They want you to know they are not gone. If you
are here ... a loved one has called on you to be here and you
have chosen to learn how to listen. Tonight, my sister will give
you your first stepping stone to feeling and hearing that special
one you feared was gone.*

While John was addressing the crowd, he was simultaneously
speaking to me. I was experiencing, firsthand, John's ability to be
in more than one place at a time. I began to feel his energetic field
ever so gently merge with mine. It was as if his hand was reaching
out to mine to assure me ...

*"Ok, Cath, it's showtime ... we're going to give them a
taste of what's yet to come. So, get grounded. We're just doing
with the audience what you and I have been doing this past
year. We've created the energetic continuum together. We've
bridged that gap and now we're going to teach others how to
do the same. The words that are about to come out of your
mouth are already vibrating ... just relax ... lift out of your
ego and let yourself catch up with your words. You're not doing
anything different than what you've been doing for the past
forty years. Except tonight we're doing it together.*

*Keep in mind ... I could have never done this when I was
down there! Why do you think they had me "study" you all
those months? You're used to speaking in public... this is just
a simple upgrade for you! My only advantage over you now
is that I don't have to battle with my ego! But tonight, we're,
for the first time, giving both sides a taste of what it's like to
bridge that gap between the physical and non-physical realms.*

It's our relationship itself that will be transmitting this experience to them. But we each have our part. You're acting as the conduit for those in the third dimension and I'm the conduit for those in the non-physical. This is what we've been schooled to teach, and tonight we're just giving them the introduction of what is yet to come. Each of them has read what we wrote. They're here for our 'Introductory Lecture' because they want what we have ... they want to hear about the step-by-step process we have created in the series that is to come.

That's the sequel, Cath, that's the most obvious next step.

His words were like that "call to service" I had experienced over three decades ago at the Harmonic Convergence. He was right. It *was* showtime. This was the performance I had been preparing for my whole career. For years, whenever I spoke publicly, I would affirm I was standing in the "beam of light" instead of the "spotlight." That was my way of lifting out of my ego and letting my Higher Self speak through me. And I knew this was different. I knew it was an upgrade of what I had already done, but I was also confident it was doable. I just had to provide the bridge needed for those in the physical to reach across the barrier of space and time, and as they did, John would be helping their loved ones reach back.

The words began to effortlessly flow out of my mouth.

"Okay so let's begin. I want to invite those of you in these first few sections ... those of you still in this third dimension ... to close your eyes ... take a deep breath. Come into the center of your being ... feel that Light within you and let that Light begin to expand. Breathe into it until the Light envelopes your whole being and extends about 9-18 inches outside your physical form

... imagine every cell in your body feels invigorated and infused with the Light ...uplifting your awareness.

Now imagine this light around you begins to form a column of Light that ascends and reaches about 60 feet above your crown chakra ... an energy center right in the middle of the top of your head ... as your awareness expands you begin to remember ... you remember a special moment when you and your loved one felt love, felt connected.

Now take another deep breath and tune into the vibration of that moment ... listen to that vibration ... listen with your heart. ... feel the pulsation of that energetic connection. Tune into it ... use the senses of this dimension to give it color, texture, smell, even sound. That will make it more real for you. Stay with that for a moment. Expand and bring it into your heart. Anchor that feeling into your heart.

This is the continuum of your love.

Be aware that your loved one on the other side can now tune into that vibration of feeling because it bridges time and space. This is where your Souls meet, commune, feel close. There is no separation when you let yourself connect beyond attachment, beyond fear. Let yourself know, feel, sense, and believe this to be true.

As you each, from your respective dimensions, extend you expand to your unique vibrational signature formed only because of the love you exchanged ... a love that enables you to simultaneously reach across the Veil to meet ... to connect. Feel that reunion as your combined intent vibrationally pulls you both to that moment ... bridging the gap between the two dimensions ... re-experiencing your shared vibration of love.

This is your vibrational signature created and supported by your mutual intent. You wouldn't be here, from either side, if you had not committed long before this to experience such a reunion. Irrespective of what the purpose is of your reunion, know that you both agreed to dissolve the separation, to resolve old wounds, to explore new possibilities.

This is how you connect and bridge the gap between the physical and non-physical. It happens Soul to Soul ... heart to heart ... that's where your vibration of love exists. And when you're able to vibrate to the frequency of love, there is no separation.

So let yourself merge ... let your hands touch and know it is this level of consciousness where your connection can be sustained ... where you can determine the agreements you may have made before you knew each other on the earth plane"

As I hear myself instructing those in both dimensions to do what I am suggesting I see John facilitating the merger and as he does the very structure of the lecture hall shifts. In varying degrees of vibration, I see those in the seen and unseen touch hands. The sections merge and stack up on each other. I instruct those in physical form to simply breathe into their heart and let themselves feel that connection of love.

Then just as suddenly as this all began, the images cease. There's no elevator ... no transition ... no parting words offered to the audience that I had assumed had gathered. Instead, John and I are transported back to Garwood's. This time I'm sipping on a cappuccino and he's sipping on his diet coke. He has that grin on his face again ... *So, how did you like that for a dress rehearsal? Pretty fricking cool, huh? That's just a preview, Cath, of what's yet to come.*

My entire body was vibrating. Not only was there no separation between John and me ... I felt 'one' with everything around me. I felt the vibration of the water, the chair I was sitting in, the foam dancing on my lips, the music reaching my ear.

I look at John with a sense of complete appreciation. "So, this is it, huh, John ... this is that gift relationships across the Veil has to offer us? This is what that elevation to the fifth dimension feels like, the elevation you on that side have to offer those of us who are willing to ride that vibrational wave of love and meet you at the Veil. *Yup... that's what we have to offer and what you and I have been schooled to teach. ...*

I take a deep breath and glance again at the calming waters of Lake Tahoe. When I bring my attention back to the table, I realize John has left and is standing in the elevator ... dressed in his Harvey suit ready for another adventure. *"You get some rest, Cath, we'll begin the sequel in a few months.* To which I reply, "Make it six!" He smiles, nods and then says, *Thanks.* "For what?" I reply. As the elevator doors begin to close and his voice begins to fade, I hear ... *thanks ... thanks for keeping me real!*

I'm left alone, but not lonely. As I sit emersed in this third dimensional world vibrating to that fifth dimension of love, I have only these parting words ...

To be continued ....

OTHER BOOKS BY CATHRYN

The Inner Child Workbook
(Available at Barnes & Noble and Amazon)

Life Beyond Confusion and Fear
…Original overview of the three stages of addiction and recovery…

Maximized
…A shamanic tale about a road trip with her dog named Max…

Which Lifetime Is This Anyway?
… A metaphysical Bible for multidimensional healing…

Soul Steps
…An innovative, 90-day program integrating body,
mind, heart, and Soul...
(Available through Amazon)

Beyond Compassion
…A program which teaches you how to
"Access your Point of Power in response to Loss" …
(Inspired by personal losses experienced by the author)

Share the Gift Series
…Introducing Taylor's signature "Interactive Tapping™" as applied to:
Attracting Intimate Relationships
Attracting Abundance
Attracting Right Livelihood
Attracting Reciprocal Partnerships

All available on Cathryn's website:
http://www.EFTForYourInnerChild.com

ABOUT THE AUTHOR

CATHRYN TAYLOR IS the author of the bestselling *Inner Child Workbook* which was published by Jeremy P. Tarcher, Inc. in 1991. Since that time, it has been translated into Dutch and Spanish, and more recently into Korean and Czech. In its 40+ printing, it can still be found on the bookshelves of Barnes and Noble as well as independent bookstores; and continues to be one of the bestselling books purchased from amazon.com on this subject. "The Inner Child Workbook" was one of five books released in the late 1980s and early '90s which popularized the concept of the inner child. It is considered a classic in the inner child field and positioned Cathryn as one of the field's leading experts. Of those five authors, Cathryn is the only one who has continued to develop and apply this concept to all areas of the personality and soul. She does so because she finds it to be invaluable both in her personal growth and in her professional work with others. This dedication earned her the honor of being referred to as, *"the mother of inner child work."* Cathryn has been conducting workshops, lectures, and classes for over three decades. She authored four additional books and five eBooks and recorded a series of lectures and YouTube videos all of which cover topics on the different stages of recovery, issues of the children within, and holistic healing. Cathryn's approach is ever-evolving — her quest for transformation—never-ending.

Cathryn was licensed in the state of California in 1979 as a Marriage and Family Therapist, was certified in Chemical Dependency in 1985 and is now licensed in the state of Minnesota as an Alcohol and Drug Counselor and as a Marriage and Family Therapist. She is also trained as a Personal Life Coach, an EMDR practitioner; a practitioner of Gary Craig's *Emotional Freedom Techniques* and is a certified EFT practitioner by EFT Master Lindsay Kenny. EFT is a self-administered form of acupressure which shows great promise in resolving stress-related issues and biochemical imbalances. These challenges originate in childhood. They, however, emerge in adulthood–not only as compulsions, addictions, and spiritual and mental challenges, but also, and perhaps more profoundly, as severe emotional traumas (such as post-traumatic-stress-disorder–PTSD, depression, anxiety, or unresolved grief). Cathryn has recently obtained certification in David Bercelli's Tension and Trauma Release Exercises, commonly referred to as TRE®. This technique completes Cathryn's healing modality. She weaves each of these additional methods of healing with her expertise of the inner child work in a very dynamic and expansive way. Her approach incorporates consultation and facilitation—assisting individuals in building the relationship between their Higher Self, their Adult self and their Children Within.

Cathryn's signature brand of tapping referred to as *Interactive Tapping*™ assists individuals in arresting addictive behaviors and in addressing all concerns of the psyche. The muscular release experienced with the Trauma Release Exercises (TRE®) supports the body's ultimate health. To obtain insight regarding the spiritual aspect of childhood traumas Cathryn acquired additional training as an Akashic Records Consultant which provides the soul's perspective on issues needing resolution. She is one of the first practitioners to merge the psychological, addictive, and spiritual perspectives with the energy therapies of EFT and TRE® to offer one of the most comprehensive modalities available.

Cathryn is well-known in the mental health community as an integrationist. She has an uncanny ability to weave all of the above methods of healing together and continues to offer on-going assistance and direction through interviews, guest appearances on summits and seminars, and her 100+ YouTube educational videos which have established Cathryn as a leading inner child and soul expert throughout the world.

Join Cathryn and John at the Veil
For a dynamic 2-hour *Akashic Records Consult*
with your deceased Loved One
Call 612.710.7720 for more Information

Made in the USA
Las Vegas, NV
09 January 2022

40972872R00142